Cakes & Cake Decorating

MANDY PRYOR

A MARTIN BOOK

CONTENTS

Published by Martin Books,
an imprint of Woodhead-Faulkner Ltd,
Fitzwilliam House, 32 Trumpington Street,
Cambridge CB2 1QY

First published 1987
© Woodhead-Faulkner Ltd
ISBN 0-85941-426-4

British Library Cataloguing in Publication Data

Pryor, Mandy
    Supercook cakes & cake decorating.
    1. Cake
    I. Title
    641.8'653   TX771

    ISBN 0-85941-426-4

INTRODUCTION

Whether you are planning a simple family tea or a more elaborate celebration, Supercook can help you produce beautiful cakes for all occasions. Ranging from basic ingredients, such as baking powder and nuts, to elaborate decorations you will find Supercook products a definite boon.

Transform the simplest cakes into the most tempting treats with angelica shapes, sugar stars, sugar flowers and marzipan fruits. Children will love the jelly diamonds, hundreds and thousands, sugar strands and orange and lemon jelly slices—none of which contain artificial colours or additives. Turn to the chapters on small cakes and family cakes for inspiring ideas.

Gâteaux can be made to look and taste particularly sumptuous with the aid of Supercook's attractive chocolate decorations, all kinds of nuts, colourings and flavourings.

For birthdays and other celebrations, you will find the simple, effective cake designs invaluable. Supercook's time-saving ready to use icings, marzipan, and icing cards really come to the fore in these recipes. For the less experienced cooks the reference section provides step-by-step guides to applying marzipan and royal icing, plus useful tips on piping and piped decorations.

For original ideas—from a simply-iced teatime sponge to a more elaborate Mickey Mouse House for a toddler—you will find this illustrated book indispensable.

COOKS' NOTES

Before starting on a recipe, always read the recipe and method through first to familiarize yourself with the procedure.

Use either metric or imperial measurements but not a combination of the two as the proportions are not interchangeable.

Preheat ovens to the specified temperature before baking, arranging the shelf position before heating.

All spoon measures are level.

Size 3 eggs are used unless large eggs are specified, which are size 2. Where a small egg is specified, use size 5.

If you prefer to use plain flour for Victoria Sandwich type cake mixtures add 3 teaspoons Supercook baking powder per 250 g (8 oz) plain flour.

SMALL CAKES

Most of these cakes can be made in an instant, and then enlivened with Supercook colourings, flavourings and toppings. The Chocolate Chip Buns and Coconut Cakes will be especially popular with children—so make sure you have enough!

CHOCOLATE CHIP BUNS

100 g (3½ oz) self-raising flour
25 g (1 oz) cocoa powder
1 teaspoon Supercook baking powder
2 large eggs, beaten
125 g (4 oz) soft margarine
125 g (4 oz) caster sugar
100 g (3½ oz) Supercook chocolate chips

TO DECORATE:
175 g (6 oz) Supercook milk chocolate cake covering
selection of Supercook decorations, e.g. chocolate flavour strands, hundreds & thousands, chocolate flakes, orange & lemon jelly slices, chocolate decorations, chocolate mini logs, walnut halves

1. Preheat oven to Gas Mark 5/190°C/375°F.
2. Sift the flour, cocoa powder and baking powder into a bowl.
3. Add the remaining ingredients, except the chocolate chips, and beat well until the mixture is smooth, pale and fluffy. Fold in the chocolate chips.
4. Divide the mixture between 18 Supercook baking cases placed on a baking tray.
5. Bake just above the centre of the oven for 15–20 minutes, until the cakes spring back when lightly pressed.
6. Leave to cool in the paper cases.
7. To decorate, melt the chocolate cake covering in a heatproof bowl placed over a pan of hot water. Spoon over the cakes to coat evenly.
8. Top with the suggested decorations. Leave to set.

Makes 18

Illustrated top: Fruity Chocolate Cup Cakes (page 6); bottom: Chocolate Chip Buns

FRUITY CHOCOLATE CUP CAKES

50 g (2 oz) self-raising flour
½ teaspoon Supercook baking
*   powder*
1 large egg, beaten
50 g (2 oz) soft margarine
50 g (2 oz) caster sugar
8 Supercook chocolate dessert
*   cups*

TO DECORATE:
1 teaspoon Supercook
*   strawberry flavouring*
*   (optional)*
300 ml (½ pint) double cream
8 fresh strawberries or cherries,
*   or other pieces of fruit in*
*   season*
4 Supercook chocolate mini logs
4 Supercook chocolate
*   decorations*

1. Preheat oven to Gas Mark 5/190°C/375°F.
2. Sift the flour and baking powder into a bowl. Add the egg, margarine and sugar and beat well until the mixture is smooth, pale and fluffy.
3. Divide the mixture between 8 Supercook baking cases placed on a baking tray.
4. Bake just above the centre of the oven for 15–20 minutes, until the cakes are golden and spring back when lightly pressed.
5. Leave to cool in the paper cases.
6. Remove the cakes from their cases and place each inside a dessert cup.
7. Stir the strawberry flavouring, if using, into the cream, then whip until stiff. Pipe or spoon into the cups.
8. Decorate each cake with a piece of fruit and top half the cakes with chocolate mini logs and half with chocolate decorations.

VARIATION

Nutty Chocolate Cup Cakes: Follow steps 1 to 6 as above. To decorate, replace the strawberry flavouring with brandy flavouring, add to the cream and whip until stiff. Omit the fruit. Instead sprinkle 40 g (1½ oz) Supercook chopped mixed nuts on a baking tray and place under a preheated moderate grill, until browned. When cool, fold the nuts into the brandy-flavoured cream. Use to fill the cases, then top with Supercook decorations.

Makes 8

Illustrated on page 5

COCONUT CAKES

125 g (4 oz) self-raising flour
½ teaspoon Supercook baking
   powder
2 large eggs, beaten
125 g (4 oz) soft margarine

125 g (4 oz) caster sugar
50 g (2 oz) desiccated coconut
1 teaspoon Supercook coconut
   flavouring

1. Preheat oven to Gas Mark 5/190°C/375°F.
2. Sift the flour and baking powder into a bowl. Add the remaining ingredients and beat well until the mixture is smooth, pale and fluffy.
3. Divide the mixture between 18 Supercook baking cases placed on a baking tray.
4. Bake just above the centre of the oven for 15–20 minutes, until the cakes are golden and spring back when lightly pressed.
5. Leave to cool in the paper cases.

VARIATIONS

Currant Cakes: Omit the coconut and flavouring. Stir 100 g (3½ oz) currants into the beaten mixture.

Iced Buns: Omit the coconut and flavouring. Decorate the cooled cakes with one quantity Glacé Icing (page 82), coloured or flavoured as wished, and assorted Supercook decorations, e.g. hundreds and thousands, jelly diamonds, sugar stars, orange and lemon jelly slices, marzipan fruits, sugar strands, chocolate flakes, chopped mixed nuts.

Makes 18

Illustrated on page 9

FONDANT FANCIES

175 g (6 oz) self-raising flour
½ teaspoon Supercook baking
   powder
3 eggs, beaten
175 g (6 oz) soft margarine
175 g (6 oz) caster sugar
grated rind of 1 orange
3 tablespoons orange juice
TO DECORATE:
2 × 350 g (12 oz) drums
   Supercook ready to use
   fondant icing

3 Supercook colourings
1 tube Supercook ready to use
   white decorating icing
selection of Supercook cake
   decorations, e.g. marzipan
   fruits, angelica, jelly
   diamonds, chocolate
   decorations, toasted flaked
   almonds

1. Grease and line an oblong cake tin, approximately 25 × 18 cm
(10 × 7 inches)—see page 81.
2. Preheat oven to Gas Mark 4/180°C/350°F.
3. Sift the flour and baking powder into a bowl. Add the remaining
ingredients and beat well until the mixture is smooth, pale and
fluffy.
4. Transfer the mixture to the prepared tin. Bake just above the
centre of the oven for 30–35 minutes, until the cake is golden and
springs back when lightly pressed.
5. Leave in the tin for a few minutes, then turn onto a wire rack to
cool, removing lining paper.
6. Cut the cake into 16 pieces: squares, triangles or circles, or a
mixture.
7. To decorate, divide the fondant icing into 3 portions. Colour each
portion a different pastel colour with the colourings. Roll out the
fondant and use to cover the cakes (see page 89). Leave to set.
8. Trim the bottom edges of each cake. Using the decorating icing
pipe a design on the top of each cake. Pipe a border around the
bottom edge of each cake if you wish.
9. Top with a variety of the suggested decorations.

Makes 16

Illustrated top: Fondant Fancies; bottom: Iced Buns (page 7)

CHOCOLATE BROWNIES

50 g (2 oz) Supercook plain
   chocolate cake covering
125 g (4 oz) butter
125 g (4 oz) plain flour
½ teaspoon Supercook baking
   powder
125 g (4 oz) caster sugar
½ teaspoon Supercook vanilla
   flavouring
1 egg, beaten
50 g (2 oz) Supercook chopped
   walnuts
1 tablespoon milk

TO DECORATE:
50 g (2 oz) Supercook plain
   chocolate cake covering
50 g (2 oz) butter
selection of Supercook
   decorations, e.g. chocolate
   mini logs, chocolate flakes,
   walnut halves, chopped
   mixed nuts

1. Grease and base-line a shallow 18 cm (7 inch) square cake tin (see pages 81).

2. Preheat oven to Gas Mark 4/180°C/350°F.

3. Melt the chocolate cake covering and butter together in a heatproof bowl placed over a pan of hot water.

4. Sift the flour, then add to the chocolate mixture with the remaining ingredients. Mix well.

5. Transfer the mixture to the prepared tin, smoothing the top. Bake on the centre shelf for 25–30 minutes, until the cake has risen and springs back when lightly pressed.

6. Turn onto a wire rack to cool, removing lining paper.

7. To decorate, melt the chocolate cake covering and butter together in a heatproof bowl placed over a pan of hot water. Leave to cool slightly until the mixture begins to thicken, then spread over the top of the cake. Mark on a pattern with a palette knife if you wish.

8. Cut the cake into 9 squares using a sharp knife, and top with the suggested decorations.

Makes 9

Illustrated on page 13

SPONGE DROPS

Plain sponge drops, without the jam and cream filling, make an ideal addition to a child's lunch box.

2 large eggs
50 g (2 oz) caster sugar
50 g (2 oz) plain flour, sifted
Supercook flaked almonds or
   sweet almonds

FOR THE FILLING (optional):
2 tablespoons raspberry jam
150 ml (¼ pint) double cream,
   whipped

1. Line 2 baking trays with Supercook rice paper.
2. Preheat oven to Gas Mark 5/190°C/375°F.
3. Whisk the eggs and sugar together in a large heatproof bowl placed over a pan of hot water until the mixture is pale in colour and the whisk leaves a trail.
4. Using a metal spoon, gently fold in the flour.
5. Spoon the mixture onto the rice paper to make 16 rounds. Place an almond on each round.
6. Bake just above the centre of the oven for 8–10 minutes, until golden.
7. Leave to cool, then cut around each cake with scissors, discarding any excess rice paper.
8. Serve the sponge drops plain or sandwich together with the jam and cream.

VARIATIONS

Lemon: Add 2 teaspoons Supercook lemon flavouring to the eggs and sugar before whisking.

Almond: Add 1½ teaspoons Supercook almond flavouring to the eggs and sugar before whisking.

Makes 16

ALMOND SLICES

175 g (6 oz) ready-made
shortcrust pastry
4 tablespoons raspberry jam,
warmed
200 g (7 oz) caster sugar
100 g (3½ oz) ground almonds
150 g (5 oz) ground rice

2 teaspoons Supercook almond
flavouring
2 eggs, beaten
TO DECORATE:
Supercook flaked almonds
Supercook sweet almonds

1. Lightly grease a shallow oblong cake tin approximately
28 × 18 cm (11 × 7 inches).
2. Preheat oven to Gas Mark 5/190°C/375°F.
3. Roll out the pastry on a floured surface to approximately
30 × 20 cm (12 × 8 inches). Line the tin with the pastry, taking it up
the sides of the tin.
4. Spread the jam over the pastry base.
5. Place the sugar, ground almonds and ground rice in a bowl.
Make a well in the centre, then add the flavouring and beaten eggs.
Mix well.
6. Spread the mixture over the pastry in the tin. Sprinkle half with
flaked almonds, the other half with sweet almonds.
7. Bake on the centre shelf for 25–30 minutes, until the pastry is
crisp and the almond mixture is crisp on top.
8. Leave to cool in the tin, then cut into 12 slices.

VARIATION

Make up a quantity of Glacé Icing (page 82); add a few drops of
Supercook almond flavouring and a few drops of Supercook pink
colouring. Drizzle over the cakes when cool. Cut into slices when
the icing has set.

Makes 12

Illustrated top: Chocolate Brownies (page 10); bottom: Almond
Slices

GINGERCAKE SQUARES

50 g (2 oz) butter or margarine
100 g (3½ oz) golden syrup
75 g (3 oz) black treacle
75 ml (3 fl oz) milk
1 egg, beaten
100 g (3½ oz) plain flour
½ teaspoon Supercook
   bicarbonate of soda

½ teaspoon ground mixed spice
1–2 teaspoons ground ginger
25 g (1 oz) caster sugar
TO DECORATE:
1 quantity Glacé Icing (page 82)
25 g (1 oz) Supercook
   crystallized ginger

1. Grease and line an 18 cm (7 inch) square cake tin (see page 81).
2. Preheat oven to Gas Mark 2/150°C/300°F.
3. In a saucepan, melt together the butter or margarine, golden syrup and black treacle; do not boil. Add the milk.
4. Leave to cool slightly, then beat in the egg.
5. Sift together the remaining ingredients, then add to the wet mixture a little at a time, beating well between each addition.
6. Pour the mixture into the prepared tin. Bake just above the centre of the oven for 30–35 minutes, until a skewer pierced through the centre of the cake comes out clean.
7. Leave in the tin for 5 minutes before turning onto a wire rack to cool.
8. Cut the cake into 9 pieces. Spread a layer of glacé icing over each and decorate with a few pieces of crystallized ginger. Leave aside until set.

Makes 9

VARIATION

Gingerbread: To make a gingerbread loaf, instead of individual cakes, grease and line a 500 g (1lb) loaf tin. Preheat the oven and make the mixture as above. Pour the mixture into the prepared loaf tin and bake above the centre of the oven for 1 hour, until a skewer pierced through the centre of the loaf comes out clean. Cool as above. Omit the decoration; instead serve in slices, with butter.

RICE AND ALMOND CRISPIES

50 g (2 oz) crisped rice
50 g (2 oz) Supercook flaked
  almonds

175 g (6 oz) Supercook milk
  chocolate cake covering
1–2 teaspoons Supercook
  coconut flavouring

1. Mix together the crisped rice and flaked almonds.
2. Melt the chocolate cake covering in a large heatproof bowl placed over a pan of hot water. Stir in the flavouring.
3. Stir the cereal mixture into the melted chocolate.
4. Spoon into 15 Supercook baking cases. Leave to cool and set.

Makes 15

CORNFLAKE AND WALNUT CRUNCHIES

75 g (3 oz) cornflakes
75 g (3 oz) Supercook walnut
  pieces

125 g (4 oz) Supercook orange
  chocolate cake covering
25 g (1 oz) butter

1. Mix together the cornflakes and walnuts.
2. Melt the chocolate cake covering and butter together in a large heatproof bowl placed over a pan of hot water.
3. Stir the cornflake mixture into the melted chocolate.
4. Spoon into 15 Supercook baking cases or about 35 Supercook mini baking cases. Leave to cool and set.

Makes 15 or 35

FAMILY CAKES

This chapter contains a variety of delicious teatime treats that the whole family will love. Included are ever-popular recipes like Date and Walnut Loaf as well as a selection of new ideas for you to try.

BANANA AND APRICOT LOAF

125 g (4 oz) plain flour
½ teaspoon Supercook
   bicarbonate of soda
¼ teaspoon salt
75 g (3 oz) butter or margarine
125 g (4 oz) caster sugar

1 large egg
150 g (5 oz) ripe banana,
   mashed
75 g (3 oz) dried apricots,
   chopped, soaked until soft,
   then drained

1. Grease and line a 500 g (1 lb) loaf tin (see page 81).
2. Preheat oven to Gas Mark 3/170°C/325°F.
3. Sift together the flour, bicarbonate of soda and salt.
4. Cream the butter or margarine and sugar together until pale and fluffy. Beat in the egg.
5. Using a metal spoon, fold in the flour mixture, banana and apricots.
6. Transfer the mixture to the prepared tin. Bake just above the centre of the oven for 1¼ hours, until a skewer pierced through the centre of the cake comes out clean.
7. Turn onto a wire rack to cool, removing lining paper.

Makes one 500 g (1 lb) loaf

Illustrated top: Banana and Apricot Loaf; middle: Date and Walnut Loaf (page 18); bottom: Spicy Cherry and Apple Loaf (page 18)

DATE AND WALNUT LOAF

350 g (12 oz) plain flour
2 teaspoons Supercook baking
   powder
½ teaspoon ground mixed spice
½ teaspoon salt
100 g (3½ oz) butter, cubed
100 g (3½ oz) light brown sugar
125 g (4 oz) dates, roughly
   chopped
75 g (3 oz) Supercook chopped
   walnuts

2 eggs, beaten
150 ml (¼ pint) milk
100 g (3½ oz) black treacle
TO DECORATE:
6 Supercook walnut halves
25 g (1 oz) glacé cherries,
   halved
few pieces Supercook angelica
1 tablespoon Apricot Glaze
   (page 86)

1. Grease and line a 1 kg (2 lb) loaf tin (see page 81).
2. Preheat oven to Gas Mark 4/180°C/350°F.
3. Sift the flour, baking powder, mixed spice and salt into a bowl. Add the butter and rub in with fingertips until the mixture resembles fine breadcrumbs.
4. Stir in the sugar, dates and walnuts. Add the remaining ingredients and mix well.
5. Transfer the mixture to the prepared tin. Bake in the centre of the oven for 1½ hours, until a skewer pierced through the centre of the cake comes out clean.
6. Turn onto a wire rack to cool, removing lining paper.
7. Decorate the top with walnuts, cherries and angelica. Brush with warm apricot glaze.
8. Serve in slices, with butter if you wish.

Makes one 1 kg (2 lb) loaf

Illustrated on page 17

SPICY CHERRY AND APPLE LOAF

250 g (8 oz) plain flour
2 teaspoons Supercook baking
   powder
½ teaspoon ground cinnamon
¼ teaspoon ground nutmeg
75 g (3 oz) butter, cubed
75 g (3 oz) caster sugar

125 g (4 oz) glacé cherries,
   chopped, rinsed and dried
50 g (2 oz) dried apple,
   chopped, soaked until soft,
   then drained
2 large eggs, beaten
75 ml (3 fl oz) milk

1. Grease and line a 1 kg (2 lb) loaf tin (see page 81).
2. Preheat oven to Gas Mark 4/180°C/350°F.
3. Sift the flour, baking powder, cinnamon and nutmeg into a bowl. Add the butter and rub in with fingertips until the mixture resembles fine breadcrumbs.
4. Stir in the sugar, cherries and apple. Add the eggs and milk and mix well.
5. Transfer the mixture to the prepared tin. Bake in the centre of the oven for 1 hour, until a skewer pierced through the centre of the cake comes out clean.
6. Turn onto a wire rack to cool, removing lining paper.
7. Serve in slices, with butter.

Makes one 1 kg (2 lb) loaf

Illustrated on page 17

SULTANA SCONES

250 g (8 oz) wholemeal flour
1 teaspoon Supercook cream of tartar
½ teaspoon Supercook bicarbonate of soda
½ teaspoon salt
50 g (2 oz) butter, cubed
25 g (1 oz) caster sugar
125 g (4 oz) sultanas
125 ml (4 fl oz) milk
milk to glaze

1. Preheat oven to Gas Mark 7/220°C/425°F.
2. Place the flour, cream of tartar, bicarbonate of soda and salt in a mixing bowl.
3. Add the butter and rub in with fingertips until the mixture resembles fine breadcrumbs.
4. Stir in the caster sugar and the sultanas. Add the milk and mix to a soft dough.
5. Knead on a lightly floured surface until smooth, then roll out to approximately 2 cm (¾ inch) thick. Using a fluted cutter, cut out approximately fourteen 5 cm (2 inch) rounds.
6. Place the scones on a floured baking tray, then brush with milk.
7. Bake just above the centre of the oven for 12–15 minutes until well risen and golden brown.
8. Transfer to a wire rack to cool. Serve warm or cold with butter.

Makes approximately 14 scones

CHESTNUT TEA RING

15 g (½ oz) fresh yeast
½ teaspoon sugar
175 ml (3 fl oz) warm milk
250 g (8 oz) strong white flour
25 g (1 oz) caster sugar
25 g (1 oz) butter or margarine
1 egg, beaten
200 g (7 oz) unsweetened
  chestnut purée
50 g (2 oz) Supercook chopped
  mixed nuts

50 g (2 oz) caster sugar
milk to glaze
TO DECORATE:
½ quantity Glacé Icing (page
  82)
25 g (1 oz) Supercook chopped
  mixed nuts

1. Add the yeast and sugar to the warm milk and leave to stand
until frothy, about 10 minutes.
2. Mix the flour and sugar together in a large bowl, then rub in the
butter or margarine with fingertips.
3. Add the yeast liquid and egg and stir to bind to a soft dough.
4. Turn onto a floured surface and knead for 10 minutes. Cover with
a tea-towel and leave to stand in a warm place for approximately
45 minutes, until doubled in size.
5. Knead again for 5 minutes, then roll out to an oblong
approximately 30 × 20 cm (12 × 8 inches).
6. Spread the chestnut purée over the dough, then sprinkle with
the nuts and sugar. Roll the dough up from a long side.
7. Lightly grease a baking tray and place the dough on it in a circle,
pushing the ends together. Make 12 cuts, at equal intervals, two
thirds of the way through the ring, leaving the centre of the ring
intact. Turn each section upwards at an angle to expose the rolled
section.
8. Cover with a tea-towel and leave in a warm place for about
1 hour, until doubled in size.
9. Meanwhile, preheat oven to Gas Mark 6/200°C/400°F.
10. Brush the ring with milk. Bake in the top third of the oven for
18–20 minutes, until the base sounds hollow when tapped.
11. Cool on a wire rack.
12. Cover the top with a layer of glacé icing, allowing it to run down
the side, and sprinkle with the chopped nuts.

Makes one large ring with 12 pieces

APPLE AND CINNAMON SCONE ROUND

This is halfway between a scone and a cake— made deliciously moist by the addition of grated apple.

200 g (7 oz) self-raising flour
1 teaspoon Supercook baking
   powder
½ teaspoon salt
1 teaspoon ground cinnamon
50 g (2 oz) butter, cubed

50 g (2 oz) caster sugar
1 medium cooking apple,
   peeled, cored and grated
50 ml (2 fl oz) milk
milk to glaze
25 g (1 oz) demerara sugar

1. Preheat oven to Gas Mark 6/200°C/400°F.
2. Sift the flour, baking powder, salt and cinnamon into a mixing bowl.
3. Add the butter and rub in with fingertips until the mixture resembles fine breadcrumbs.
4. Stir in the caster sugar and apple. Add the milk and mix to a dough.
5. Knead on a lightly floured surface until smooth, then shape into a 20 cm (8 inch) round on a floured baking tray.
6. Brush with milk and sprinkle with the demerara sugar. Mark into 10 sections with a sharp knife.
7. Bake just above the centre of the oven for 20–25 minutes.
8. Serve hot or cold, with butter.

Makes one 20 cm (8 inch) cake

VICTORIA SANDWICH

175 g (6 oz) butter or margarine
175 g (6 oz) caster sugar
3 eggs, beaten
175 g (6 oz) self-raising flour,
   sifted

TO FINISH:
3 tablespoons jam (e.g.
   raspberry, strawberry,
   apricot)
1 tablespoon caster sugar

1. Grease and base-line two 18 cm (7 inch) sandwich tins (see page 81).
2. Preheat oven to Gas Mark 4/180°C/350°F.
3. Cream the butter or margarine and sugar together until pale and fluffy.
4. Beat in the eggs, one at a time; if the mixture begins to curdle, add a tablespoon of the flour with the second egg.
5. Using a metal spoon, gently fold in the flour.
6. Divide the mixture between the prepared tins and bake just above the centre of the oven for 25–30 minutes, until the cakes are golden and spring back when lightly pressed.
7. Turn onto a wire rack to cool, removing lining paper.
8. Sandwich the cakes together with the jam. Sprinkle the caster sugar over the top.

VARIATIONS

Iced Victoria Sandwich: Top the cake with 1 quantity lemon-flavoured Glacé Icing (page 82). Place a row of Supercook sugar stars around the edge.

Brandy and Chocolate Cake: Make up 1 quantity brandy-flavoured Butter Icing (page 82). Use two thirds of it to sandwich the cake together, in place of the jam. Pipe a row of stars around the top edge of the cake using the remaining butter cream and place a Supercook chocolate decoration on each star.

Makes one 18 cm (7 inch) cake

CARIBBEAN TEA RING

Shredded coconut gives this cake an especially good texture—if unavailable you can substitute desiccated coconut.

125 g (4 oz) butter or margarine
125 g (4 oz) caster sugar
2 eggs, beaten
100 g (3½ oz) self-raising flour, sifted
50 g (2 oz) glacé pineapple pieces (chopped if large)
40 g (1½ oz) shredded tenderized coconut

1 tablespoon Supercook rum flavouring
TO DECORATE:
1 quantity coconut Glacé Icing (page 82)
few pieces glacé pineapple
few pieces Supercook angelica

1. Grease and flour a 20 cm (8 inch) ring mould.
2. Preheat oven to Gas Mark 4/180°C/350°F.
3. Cream the butter or margarine and sugar together until pale and fluffy.
4. Beat in the eggs, one at a time; if the mixture begins to curdle, add a tablespoon of the flour.
5. Using a metal spoon, fold in the flour and remaining ingredients.
6. Transfer the mixture to the prepared tin and bake just above the centre of the oven for 20–25 minutes, until the cake has risen and springs back when lightly pressed.
7. Turn onto a wire rack to cool.
8. To decorate, pour the glacé icing over the cake, allowing it to run down the side. Arrange pieces of pineapple and angelica on top.

Makes one 20 cm (8 inch) cake

Illustrated on page 25

UPSIDE-DOWN APPLE GINGERCAKE

50 g (2 oz) butter, melted
25 g (1 oz) caster sugar
1 large cooking apple, peeled,
    cored and sliced
125 g (4 oz) self-raising flour
1½ teaspoons ground ginger
½ teaspoon ground nutmeg

125 g (4 oz) butter or margarine
125 g (4 oz) light brown sugar
grated rind and juice of 1 small
    lemon
2 eggs, beaten
50 g (2 oz) Supercook
    crystallized ginger

1. Preheat oven to Gas Mark 4/180°C/350°F.
2. Grease and base-line a deep 18 cm (7 inch) round cake tin (see page 81). Pour the melted butter into the tin and sprinkle the caster sugar evenly on top.
3. Arrange the apple slices over the butter and sugar.
4. Sift together the flour, ginger and nutmeg.
5. Cream the butter or margarine and brown sugar together until pale and fluffy. Beat in the lemon rind and juice.
6. Beat in the eggs, one at a time; if the mixture begins to curdle, add a tablespoon of the flour with the second egg.
7. Using a metal spoon, fold in the flour mixture and the crystallized ginger.
8. Pour the mixture onto the apple. Bake in the centre of the oven for 50–60 minutes, until the cake has risen and springs back when lightly pressed.
9. Turn straight out onto a serving plate. Serve hot with single or whipped cream as a dessert, or cold at tea time.

Makes one 18 cm (7 inch) cake

Illustrated top: Upside-down Apple Gingercake; bottom:
Caribbean Tea Ring (page 23)

SWISS ROLL

3 large eggs
75 g (3 oz) caster sugar
75 g (3 oz) plain flour, sifted

TO FINISH:
4 tablespoons raspberry jam,
    warmed
1 tablespoon caster sugar

1. Grease and line a 20 × 30 cm (8 × 12 inch) Swiss roll tin (see page 81).
2. Preheat oven to Gas Mark 6/200°C/400°F.
3. Whisk the eggs and sugar together in a heatproof bowl placed over a pan of hot water, until the mixture is pale in colour and the whisk leaves a trail.
4. Using a metal spoon, gently fold in the flour.
5. Pour the mixture into the prepared tin. Tip the tin so that the mixture spreads evenly.
6. Bake just above the centre of the oven for 8–10 minutes, until the cake is golden and springs back when lightly pressed.
7. Immediately turn out onto sugared greaseproof paper. Peel off lining paper and trim the edges of the cake to neaten.
8. Quickly spread with the jam, then roll up, starting from a short edge.
9. Transfer to a wire rack to cool, then sprinkle with caster sugar to serve.

Makes one Swiss roll

CHOCOLATE AND WALNUT SWISS ROLL

3 large eggs
75 g (3 oz) caster sugar
65 g (2½ oz) plain flour, sifted
15 g (½ oz) cocoa powder,
    sifted
50 g (2 oz) Supercook walnut
    pieces, ground

TO FINISH:
1 quantity Butter Icing (page 82)
25 g (1 oz) Supercook walnut
    pieces
icing sugar to dredge

1. Make and bake the Swiss roll as above, folding in the cocoa and walnut pieces with the flour.
2. Immediately turn out onto sugared greaseproof paper. Peel off lining paper and trim the edges of the cake to neaten.

3. Starting from a short edge, roll the cake up with the greaseproof paper. Transfer to a wire rack to cool.
4. Carefully unroll the cake, spread with the butter icing and sprinkle with the walnuts. Roll the cake up again and dredge with icing sugar.

Makes one Swiss roll

MARBLED NEAPOLITAN CAKE

175 g (6 oz) self-raising flour
1 teaspoon Supercook baking
  powder
175 g (6 oz) soft margarine
175 g (6 oz) caster sugar
3 eggs, beaten
½ tablespoon Supercook
  strawberry flavouring

few drops Supercook pink
  colouring
25 g (1 oz) cocoa powder, sifted
½ tablespoon milk
icing sugar to dredge

1. Grease and flour a fluted 20 cm (8 inch) round cake tin.
2. Preheat oven to Gas Mark 4/180°C/350°F.
3. Sift the flour and baking powder into a bowl.
4. Add the margarine, sugar and eggs and beat well until the mixture is smooth, pale and fluffy.
5. Divide the mixture between 3 bowls. Leave one portion plain. Add the strawberry flavouring and pink colouring to the second portion. Add the cocoa powder and milk to the third portion.
6. Place all 3 portions in one bowl and gently swirl together to create a marbled effect.
7. Transfer the mixture to the prepared tin. Bake in the centre of the oven for 1 hour, until a skewer pierced through the centre of the cake comes out clean.
8. Leave in the tin for a few minutes, then turn onto a wire rack to cool.
9. Dredge with icing sugar to serve.

Makes one 20 cm (8 inch) cake

GÂTEAUX

There is nothing quite like a luscious homemade gâteau for a special treat. Cherry and brandy, blackcurrant and rum, orange and chocolate or peach and almond—these gâteaux should tempt everyone.

BLACK FOREST BRANDY GÂTEAU

150 g (5 oz) self-raising flour
25 g (1 oz) cocoa powder
1 teaspoon Supercook baking powder
175 g (6 oz) soft margarine
175 g (6 oz) caster sugar
3 eggs, beaten
2 tablespoons Supercook brandy flavouring

TO DECORATE:
400 g (14 oz) can black cherry pie filling
2 teaspoons Supercook brandy flavouring
300 ml (½ pint) double cream
50 g (2 oz) Supercook chocolate flakes
8 Supercook chocolate decorations (optional)

1. Grease and base-line two 18 cm (7 inch) sandwich tins (see page 81).
2. Preheat oven to Gas Mark 4/180°C/350°F.
3. Sift the flour, cocoa and baking powder into a bowl.
4. Add the remaining ingredients and beat well until smooth, pale and fluffy.
5. Divide the mixture between the prepared tins. Bake just above the centre of the oven for 25–30 minutes, until the cakes spring back when lightly pressed.
6. Turn onto a wire rack to cool, removing lining paper.
7. Sandwich the cakes together with half the cherry pie filling.
8. To decorate, stir the brandy flavouring into the cream, then whip until stiff. Coat the side of the cake with half the cream.
9. Holding the cake at an angle, apply the chocolate flakes to the side with a palette knife. Place the cake on a serving plate.
10. Pipe a border on top of the cake using the remaining cream. Finish with the remaining black cherry pie filling, and the chocolate decorations if using.

Makes one 18 cm (7 inch) cake

*Illustrated top: Black Forest Brandy Gâteau;
bottom: Coffee and Nut Gâteau (page 30)*

COFFEE AND NUT GÂTEAU

4 large eggs
125 g (4 oz) caster sugar
125 g (4 oz) plain flour, sifted
50 g (2 oz) Supercook chopped
    mixed nuts
1 teaspoon Supercook coffee
    flavouring

TO DECORATE:
2 quantities coffee Butter Icing
    (page 82)
50 g (2 oz) Supercook chopped
    mixed nuts, toasted
Supercook coffee flavour
    strands

1. Grease and line a deep 23 cm (9 inch) round cake tin (see page 81).
2. Preheat oven to Gas Mark 5/190°C/375°F.
3. Whisk the eggs and sugar together in a large heatproof bowl placed over a pan of hot water, until the mixture is pale in colour and the whisk leaves a trail.
4. Using a metal spoon, gently fold in the flour, nuts and flavouring.
5. Transfer the mixture to the prepared tin. Bake in the centre of the oven for 40–45 minutes, until the cake springs back when lightly pressed and has left the side of the tin.
6. Leave in the tin for a few minutes, then turn onto a wire rack to cool, removing lining paper.
7. Cut the cake horizontally in half, then sandwich together again with a third of the butter icing.
8. Using half the remaining butter icing, spread a thin layer over the side of the cake. Spread the chopped nuts on a plate and roll the cake on its side over them to coat.
9. Place the cake on a serving plate. Coat the top with half the remaining butter icing, smoothing well.
10. To decorate the top of the cake, pipe on rows of shells at equal intervals using the remaining butter icing. Sprinkle the coffee flavour strands in between the lines of piping.

Makes one 23 cm (9 inch) cake

Illustrated on page 29

BLACKCURRANT AND RUM GÂTEAU

125 g (4 oz) butter or margarine
125 g (4 oz) caster sugar
2 eggs, beaten
125 g (4 oz) self-raising flour,
    sifted
1 tablespoon Supercook rum
    flavouring

400 g (14 oz) can blackcurrant
    pie filling
TO DECORATE:
1 teaspoon Supercook rum
    flavouring
150 ml (5 fl oz) double cream

1. Grease and line a deep loose-bottom 15 cm (6 inch) round cake tin (see page 81).
2. Preheat oven to Gas Mark 4/180°C/350°F.
3. Cream the butter or margarine and sugar together until pale and fluffy.
4. Beat in the eggs, one at a time; if the mixture begins to curdle add a tablespoon of the flour.
5. Using a metal spoon, fold in the flour and rum flavouring.
6. Place half the cake mixture in the prepared tin and level the surface. Add half the blackcurrant pie filling, spreading evenly over the cake mixture. Cover with the remaining cake mixture.
7. Bake in the centre of the oven for 1 hour, until the cake has risen, is golden and springs back when lightly pressed.
8. Turn onto a wire rack to cool.
9. Gently remove the lining paper and transfer the cake to a serving plate.
10. Stir the rum flavouring into the cream, then whip until stiff. Pipe rosettes around the top edge of the cake. Fill the centre with the remaining blackcurrant pie filling.

Makes one 15 cm (6 inch) cake

ORANGE CHOCOLATE GÂTEAU

150 g (5 oz) self-raising flour
25 g (1 oz) cocoa powder
175 g (6 oz) butter or margarine
175 g (6 oz) caster sugar
3 eggs, beaten
grated rind of 1 orange
3 tablespoons freshly-squeezed
  orange juice

TO DECORATE:
¼ teaspoon Supercook
  chocolate colouring
150 ml (5 fl oz) double cream
175 g (6 oz) Supercook orange
  chocolate cake covering
16 Supercook orange jelly slices

1. Grease and base-line two 18 cm (7 inch) sandwich tins (see page 81).
2. Preheat oven to Gas Mark 4/180°C/350°F.
3. Sift together the flour and cocoa powder.
4. Cream the butter or margarine and sugar together until pale and fluffy.
5. Beat in the eggs, one at a time; if the mixture begins to curdle, add a tablespoon of the flour mixture.
6. Using a metal spoon, fold in the flour mixture, orange rind and juice.
7. Divide the mixture between the prepared tins. Bake just above the centre of the oven for 25–30 minutes, until the cakes spring back when lightly pressed.
8. Turn onto a wire rack to cool, removing lining paper.
9. To decorate, stir the chocolate colouring into the cream, then whip until stiff. Sandwich the cakes together with half the cream.
10. Melt the chocolate cake covering in a large heatproof bowl placed over a pan of hot water. Using a palette knife, coat the side of the cake with a layer of chocolate cake covering. Spoon the remaining covering over the top of the cake and smooth over with a knife dipped in hot water. Leave to set.
11. Pipe the remaining cream in rosettes around the top edge. Decorate with the orange jelly slices.

Makes one 18 cm (7 inch) cake

Illustrated top: Lemon Cream Gâteau (page 34); bottom: Orange Chocolate Gâteau

LEMON CREAM GÂTEAU

175 g (6 oz) self-raising flour
1 teaspoon Supercook baking
   powder
175 g (6 oz) soft margarine
175 g (6 oz) caster sugar
3 eggs, beaten
2 tablespoons Supercook lemon
   flavouring

TO FILL AND DECORATE:
1 egg
125 g (4 oz) caster sugar
grated rind of 1 lemon
25 g (1 oz) cornflour
juice of 1 lemon, made up to
   150 ml (¼ pint) with water
600 ml (1 pint) whipping cream,
   whipped
4 Supercook chocolate mini logs
8 Supercook lemon jelly slices

1. Grease and base-line two 20 cm (8 inch) sandwich tins (see page 81).
2. Preheat oven to Gas Mark 4/180°C/350°F.
3. Sift the flour and baking powder into a bowl.
4. Add the remaining ingredients and beat until smooth, pale and fluffy.
5. Transfer to the prepared tins and bake just above the centre of the oven for 25–30 minutes, until the cakes are golden and spring back when lightly pressed.
6. Turn onto a wire rack to cool, removing lining paper.
7. To prepare the filling, whisk the egg, sugar and lemon rind together in a heatproof bowl placed over a pan of hot water until foamy.
8. Blend the cornflour with the lemon juice and water, then beat into the egg mixture.
9. Transfer the mixture to a saucepan and gently bring to the boil, stirring continuously. Cook for 5–7 minutes, still stirring. Leave to cool.
10. Fold in the whipped cream, then sandwich the cakes together with a third of the mixture.
11. Coat the cake with two thirds of the remaining lemon cream. Use a palette knife to make a pattern on top.
12. Crush the mini logs and press around the side of the cake.
13. Pipe the remaining cream around the top edge and arrange the jelly slices on top to decorate.

Makes one 20 cm (8 inch) cake

Illustrated on page 33

PEACH AND ALMOND GÂTEAU

4 large eggs
125 g (4 oz) caster sugar
50 g (2 oz) butter
125 g (4 oz) plain flour, sifted

TO FILL AND DECORATE:
300 ml (½ pint) whipping cream
2 teaspoons icing sugar
2 ripe peaches, stoned
75 g (3 oz) Supercook flaked
almonds, toasted

1. Grease and line a deep 23 cm (9 inch) cake tin (see page 81).
2. Preheat oven to Gas Mark 5/190°C/375°F.
3. Whisk the eggs and sugar together in a large heatproof bowl placed over a pan of hot water, until the mixture is pale in colour and thick enough to leave a trail.
4. Warm the butter gently until just melted.
5. Using a metal spoon, gently fold the flour into the egg mixture.
6. Fold in the butter carefully to avoid knocking out the air.
7. Turn the mixture into the prepared tin and bake on the centre shelf for 35–40 minutes until the cake is golden and springs back when lightly pressed.
8. After a few minutes, turn out onto a wire rack to cool.
9. Using a sharp knife, split the cake horizontally in two rounds.
10. Whip the cream with the icing sugar until stiff.
11. Chop one of the peaches roughly and fold into a third of the whipped cream. Use to sandwich the cake rounds together.
12. Coat the side and top of the cake with half the remaining cream.
13. Press the toasted flaked almonds evenly around the side of the cake.
14. Mark a pattern on top of the gâteau with a palette knife. Pipe the remaining cream around the top edge to decorate. Slice the remaining peach and arrange on top.

Makes one 23 cm (9 inch) cake

Illustrated on page 37

SUMMER CHOUX RING

300 ml (½ pint) water
100 g (3½ oz) butter
150 g (5 oz) plain flour, sifted
4 eggs, beaten
25 g (1 oz) Supercook flaked
   almonds
TO FINISH:
1 teaspoon Supercook
   strawberry flavouring
   (optional)

300 ml (½ pint) double cream
500 g (1 lb) fresh raspberries or
   strawberries (halved if large)
icing sugar to dredge
raspberry or strawberry leaves
   (if available)

1. Line 2 baking trays with greaseproof paper. Draw a 20 cm (8 inch) circle on each, then grease lightly.
2. Preheat oven to Gas Mark 6/200°C/400°F.
3. Place the water and butter in a saucepan and bring to the boil. As soon as the liquid boils, add the flour and beat thoroughly until smooth. Cook for 2–3 minutes.
4. Leave to cool slightly, then beat in the eggs a little at a time.
5. Spread two thirds of the mixture into a round within the marked circle on one baking tray. Spoon the remaining mixture onto the other tray to form a ring within the marked circle. Sprinkle the flaked almonds over the ring.
6. Bake in the top third of the oven; the ring for 30–35 minutes and the round for 35–40 minutes, until well risen and crisp.
7. As soon as they are removed from the oven, pierce the pastry to allow steam to escape. Turn onto a wire rack to cool.
8. Stir the strawberry flavouring, if using, into the cream, then whip until stiff. Spread over the round.
9. Place some of the fruit over the cream. Place the pastry ring on top and pile the remaining fruit in the centre.
10. Dredge with icing sugar, then decorate with the raspberry or strawberry leaves, if using.

Makes one 20 cm (8 inch) cake

Illustrated top: Summer Choux Ring; bottom: Peach and Almond Gâteau (page 35)

BUTTERSCOTCH MILLEFEUILLE GÂTEAU

500 g (1 lb) ready-made puff
pastry
1 egg, beaten, to glaze
icing sugar to dredge
BUTTERSCOTCH CREAM:
400 ml (14 fl oz) milk

100 g (3½ oz) caster sugar
4 egg yolks
50 g (2 oz) plain flour
2 teaspoons Supercook
butterscotch flavouring

1. Roll out the pastry on a floured surface to approximately 3 mm (⅛ inch) thickness. Cut into 4 oblongs measuring approximately 23 × 15 cm (9 × 6 inches) and place on 2 dampened baking trays. Knock up the edges with a sharp knife to encourage flaking. Cover with clingfilm and chill for 30 minutes.
2. To make the butterscotch cream, heat the milk to scalding point.
3. Cream the sugar and egg yolks together, then beat in the flour.
4. Stir in the milk, then return the mixture to the saucepan. Bring slowly to the boil and cook for 2 minutes, stirring continuously.
5. Add the butterscotch flavouring, cover with clingfilm and leave to cool.
6. Preheat oven to Gas Mark 7/220°C/425°F.
7. Brush the pastry strips with beaten egg and bake in the top third of the oven for 15–20 minutes, until well risen and golden brown.
8. Transfer to a wire rack to cool.
9. Sandwich the pastry layers together with the butterscotch cream, finishing with pastry. Dredge with icing sugar.

VARIATION

Raspberry and Nut Millefeuille Gâteau: Omit the butterscotch cream; instead toast 50 g (2 oz) Supercook chopped mixed nuts under a moderate grill until browned. Leave to cool. Whip 300 ml (½ pint) double cream until stiff, then fold in the nuts. Spread 3 tablespoons of raspberry jam over 3 pastry layers. Sandwich, together with the nut cream, finishing with the remaining pastry layer.

Makes one 23 × 15 cm (9 × 6 inch) cake

PINEAPPLE MERINGUE GÂTEAU

4 large egg whites
200 g (7 oz) caster sugar
few drops Supercook yellow
  colouring
1 tablespoon Supercook lemon
  flavouring

400 g (14 oz) can pineapple
  pieces, drained
300 ml (½ pint) whipping
  cream, whipped
few pieces Supercook angelica

1. Line 3 baking trays with baking parchment. Draw a 20 cm
(8 inch) circle on each.
2. Preheat oven to Gas Mark 1/140°C/275°F.
3. In a large bowl, whisk the egg whites until stiff.
4. Add half the sugar and the colouring and continue to whisk until
very stiff.
5. Using a metal spoon, fold in the remaining sugar and the lemon
flavouring.
6. Spread the mixture evenly over the 3 rounds.
7. Bake for about 1½ hours so that the meringue is dry on the
outside but still a little soft in the centre.
8. Transfer to a wire rack to cool, carefully peeling off the baking
parchment.
9. Reserve about 8 pineapple pieces for decoration; fold the
remainder into two thirds of the whipped cream.
10. Place one of the meringue rounds on a serving plate and
spread over half the cream mixture. Top with another meringue
round and spread over the remaining cream mixture.
11. Position the final meringue round on top. Use the remaining
whipped cream to pipe a border around the top edge.
12. Decorate with the reserved pineapple pieces and tiny pieces
of angelica.

Makes one 20 cm (8 inch) cake

NOVELTY CAKES

In this chapter you will find ideas for all members of the family. The Butterfly (page 44) would make a lovely birthday cake for a girl and any small boy would love the Train cake on page 56.

Cakes covered with sugar paste and fondant icing should be left in a warm, dry place for 24 hours before decorating. Apply the final decorations on the day the cake is required, if possible.

DICE

150 g (5 oz) self-raising flour
25 g (1 oz) cocoa powder
1 teaspoon Supercook baking
    powder
3 eggs, beaten
175 g (6 oz) soft margarine
175 g (6 oz) caster sugar

TO DECORATE:
5 tablespoons Apricot Glaze
    (page 86)
500 g (1 lb) Supercook ready to
    use fondant icing
1 drum Supercook chocolate
    chips

1. Grease and line a deep 25 × 18 cm (10 × 7 inch) oblong cake tin (see page 81).
2. Preheat oven to Gas Mark 4/180°C/350°F.
3. Sift the flour, cocoa powder and baking powder into a bowl.
4. Add the remaining ingredients and beat until pale and fluffy.
5. Transfer the mixture to the prepared tin. Bake just above the centre of the oven for 30–35 minutes, until the cake springs back when lightly pressed.
6. Turn onto a wire rack to cool, removing lining paper.
7. Cut into 16 pieces and brush each piece with apricot glaze.
8. Divide the fondant icing into sixteen, roll out and use to cover the cakes (see page 89).
9. Attach the chocolate chips to the cakes with apricot glaze to resemble dice. Leave until firm.

Makes 16

Illustrated opposite: Mickey Mouse House (page 42); below: Dice

MICKEY MOUSE© HOUSE

175 g (6 oz) butter or margarine
175 g (6 oz) caster sugar
3 eggs, beaten
175 g (6 oz) self-raising flour,
  sifted
1 tablespoon Supercook
  coconut flavouring
75 g (3 oz) desiccated coconut
TO DECORATE:
1 tablespoon apricot jam
1 quantity Butter Icing (page 82)
1 drum Supercook hundreds
  and thousands

1 drum Supercook jelly
  diamonds
4 Supercook Mickey Mouse©
  edible wafers
1 tube Supercook ready to use
  chocolate decorating icing
2 Supercook silver balls
75 g (3 oz) desiccated coconut
several drops Supercook green
  food colouring
1 drum Supercook sugar stars
1 box Supercook mini logs

1. Grease and line a 500 g (1 lb) and a 1 kg (2 lb) loaf tin of the same length (see page 81).
2. Preheat oven to Gas Mark 4/180°C/350°F.
3. Cream the butter or margarine and sugar together until pale and fluffy.
4. Beat in the eggs, one at a time; if the mixture begins to curdle add a tablespoon of the flour with the second egg.
5. Fold in the flour and remaining ingredients.
6. Place one third of the mixture in the smaller tin, the rest in the larger tin. Bake just above the centre of the oven for 35–40 minutes for the smaller cake and 50–60 minutes for the larger, until the cakes spring back when lightly pressed.
7. Turn onto a wire rack to cool, removing lining papers.
8. Trim each side of the smaller cake to a point, making a roof shape. Sandwich the roof to the larger cake with the jam and place on a Supercook 25 cm (10 inch) square board.
9. Set aside a third of the butter icing; coat the whole cake with the remainder.
10. Push hundreds and thousands onto both ends of the house to resemble pebble dashing. Place the jelly diamonds on the roof to resemble tiles. Stick the wafers to the front and back of the cake.
11. Using the writing or leaf nozzle on the chocolate icing tube, draw windows and doors. Add a silver ball to each door as a handle.
12. Tint the reserved butter icing green and spread over the cake board. Tint the coconut green and sprinkle over the butter icing for grass. Use the remaining hundreds and thousands to make a path.
13. Position the sugar stars for flowers. Halve the mini logs and use to represent a chimney and a fence.

BIRD'S NEST

75 g (3 oz) self-raising flour
25 g (1 oz) cocoa powder
½ teaspoon Supercook baking
  powder
125 g (4 oz) soft margarine
125 g (4 oz) caster sugar
2 eggs, beaten

TO DECORATE:
100 g (3½ oz) Supercook plain
  chocolate cake covering
1 quantity Butter Icing (page 82)
few drops Supercook chocolate
  colouring
3 Supercook chocolate
  decorations
2 Supercook chocolate chips
2 Supercook jelly diamonds

1. Grease and flour a 20 cm (8 inch) ring mould.
2. Preheat oven to Gas Mark 4/180°C/350°F.
3. Sift the flour, cocoa powder and baking powder into a bowl.
4. Add the remaining ingredients and beat until smooth, pale and fluffy.
5. Place 1 teaspoon of the mixture into each of 4 Supercook baking cases. Place the remaining mixture in the ring mould. Bake just above the centre of the oven for 15–20 minutes for the small cakes and 25–30 minutes for the ring mould, until the cakes spring back when lightly pressed.
6. Turn onto a wire rack to cool.
7. Melt the chocolate cake covering in a heatproof bowl placed over a pan of hot water. Pour it onto the back of a baking tray, spreading thinly. Leave to set in a cool place.
8. Sandwich each pair of buns together with butter icing for the bird's head and body. Coat with butter icing and stick together to form the bird.
9. Scrape a sharp knife across the set chocolate at an angle using a sawing motion, to form long curls (caraque).
10. Colour the remaining butter icing chocolate using the colouring and use to coat the ring cake, then press on the chocolate caraque to cover.
11. Transfer the cake to a serving plate. Fill the centre with the remaining caraque.
12. Sit the bird in the nest. Attach the chocolate decorations to form the wings and tail, the chocolate chips for the eyes and the diamonds as the beak.

Mickey Mouse House illustrated on page 41

BUTTERFLY

2 mini chocolate Swiss rolls
1 unfilled Victoria sandwich
(page 22)
1 quantity Butter Icing (page 82)
few drops Supercook pink
colouring
1 drum Supercook hundreds
and thousands

1 tube Supercook ready to use
pink decorating icing
1 drum Supercook sugar stars
1 drum Supercook jelly
diamonds
4 Supercook chocolate chips
2 Supercook chocolate
decorations

1. Place the 2 mini chocolate Swiss rolls end to end on a cake board, for the butterfly's body.
2. Cut both sandwich cakes according to Fig. i, for the butterfly's wings.
3. Tint the butter icing pink, using the colouring. Reserve a teaspoon of butter icing, then use the remainder to cover the top and sides of the wings.
4. Coat the sides of the wings with hundreds and thousands, then position the wings by the body.
5. Mark a pattern on top of the wings using a palette knife. Using the writing nozzle on the pink icing tube, outline the wings with a row of dots.
6. Make a pattern on the wings using the sugar stars and jelly diamonds.
7. Using the reserved butter icing, attach the chocolate chips, and the chocolate decorations for antennae, to the body.

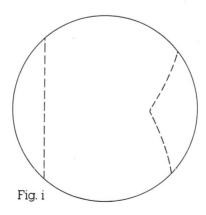

Fig. i

Illustrated top: Butterfly; bottom: Wise Owl (page 46)

WISE OWL

1 unfilled Victoria sandwich
(page 22)
1 tablespoon apricot jam
2 quantities lemon Glacé Icing
(page 82)
1 tube Supercook chocolate
ready to use decorating icing

1 drum Supercook chocolate
flakes
50 g (2 oz) Supercook marzipan
few drops Supercook yellow
colouring (optional)

---

1. Cut an arc shape, 5 cm (2 inches) in diameter, from an edge of
one of the cakes and reserve (Fig. i). Arrange the 2 cakes on a
board to resemble a head and body. Cut the reserved piece of
cake in half and trim to represent ears. Join all the pieces of cake
together with the jam (Fig. ii).
2. Cover the whole cake with the glacé icing, smoothing with a
palette knife dipped in hot water.
3. Using the writing nozzle on the chocolate icing tube,
immediately pipe parallel lines horizontally across the cake in the
area of the forehead and body. Quickly draw the point of a knife
vertically—in one direction and then in the opposite direction—at
equal intervals down the cake to form a feather effect (see page 83).
4. Pipe 2 lines over the body to form wings, then pipe on the eyes
and beak. Sprinkle chocolate flakes over the wings and ears.
5. Colour the marzipan yellow (if you wish), kneading in the
colouring well. Roll into 6 sausage shapes with your hands and
place 3 each side at the base to form feet.
6. Leave the cake to dry, then wipe around the bottom edge to tidy.

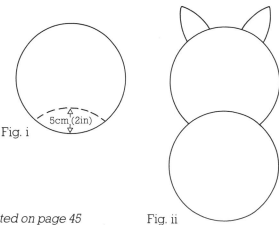

Fig. i

5cm (2in)

Illustrated on page 45

Fig. ii

PINK PIG

1 Victoria sandwich mixture
(page 22)
1 tablespoon Supercook
strawberry flavouring
4 tablespoons Apricot Glaze
(page 86)

1 quantity Sugar Paste, coloured
pink (page 88)
4 Supercook chocolate chips

1. Grease and flour two 1.2 litre (2 pint) pudding basins.
2. Preheat oven to Gas Mark 4/180°C/350°F.
3. Place the Victoria sandwich mixture in a bowl and stir in the strawberry flavouring.
4. Place a heaped teaspoon of the strawberry sponge mixture in 2 Supercook baking cases. Divide the remaining mixture between the basins, making a slight hollow in the top of each.
5. Bake just above the centre of the oven for 20–25 minutes for the small cakes and 50–55 minutes for the large, until they spring back when lightly pressed.
6. Turn the cakes onto a wire rack to cool.
7. Sandwich the 2 basin cakes together with apricot glaze. Stick one of the buns on the front as a nose. Cut the other bun in half and stick onto the cake as ears.
8. Brush the cake all over with apricot glaze.
9. Roll out the sugar paste and use to cover the cake, moulding over the nose and ears, and joining underneath (see page 89). Reserve the trimmings.
10. Stick 2 chocolate chips on the nose as nostrils and use 2 for the eyes.
11. Roll remaining paste into 4 balls for feet; position on a board. Stand the pig on these and stick in a pipe cleaner 'tail', if wished.
12. Set aside to dry. Remove the 'tail' before serving.

PIERROT CLOWN

1 'Flower Basket' birthday cake,
  undecorated (page 59)
3 tablespoons Apricot Glaze
  (page 86)
1 quantity Sugar Paste (page 88)
50 g (2 oz) Supercook plain
  chocolate cake covering

1 tube each Supercook
  chocolate, blue and red
  ready to use decorating icing
1 Supercook chocolate mini log,
  crushed

1. Make and bake the cake following steps 1 to 6 on page 59.
2. When cool, brush the cake with the apricot glaze.
3. Roll out the sugar paste and use to cover the cake (see page 89).
4. Melt the cake covering in a heatproof bowl placed over a pan of hot water. Dip a fine paintbrush in the melted chocolate and draw a line about a third of the way down across the cake to denote the edge of the cap.
5. Fill the area above the line with the melted chocolate, spreading with a palette knife and taking it down the side of the cake. Leave to dry.
6. Using the writing nozzle on the chocolate icing tube, draw in the eyes, eyelashes and nose.
7. Using the writing nozzle on the blue icing tube, draw in a tear drop just below one eye.
8. Using the writing nozzle on the red icing tube, draw in the lips.
9. Sprinkle the crushed minilog down each side from the cap to represent hair.
10. Attach a consertina folded Supercook cake frill to the bottom of the cake as a clown's ruff. Set aside to dry.

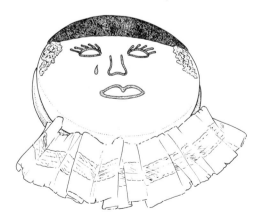

CANDLE CAKE

1 baked Swiss roll (page 26)
3 tablespoons Apricot Glaze
 (page 86)
500 g (1 lb) Supercook ready to
 use fondant icing

few drops each Supercook
 yellow and blue colouring
1 Supercook icing card with
 blue Happy Birthday lettering

1. Turn the cake onto a wire rack to cool, removing lining paper.
2. Place the cake on a work surface and cut out a candle shape with
a flame as shown in Fig. i. Assemble on a board as shown in Fig. ii.
Brush the cake with apricot glaze.
3. Take 75 g (3 oz) of the fondant icing and knead in some yellow
colouring on a surface sprinkled with cornflour until evenly
coloured. Roll out and use to cover the flame part of the cake (see
page 89).
4. In the same way, colour the remaining icing blue and use to
cover the candle part of the cake.
5. Using the icing card as instructed, place the words 'Happy
Birthday' along one side of the candle and the child's name along
the other side.
6. Finish with Supercook candles in their holders down the centre
of the cake. Set aside to dry.

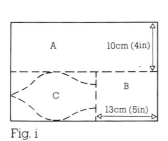

Fig. i

Fig. ii

BOWLING GREEN

175 g (6 oz) butter, softened
175 g (6 oz) caster sugar
3 eggs, beaten
175 g (6 oz) self-raising flour,
  sifted
1 tablespoon Supercook almond
  flavouring
TO DECORATE:
1 quantity Sugar Paste (page 88)

25 g (1 oz) each Supercook plain
  and milk chocolate cake
  coverings
3 tablespoons Apricot Glaze
  (page 86)
few drops Supercook green
  colouring
1 tube each Supercook
  chocolate and white ready to
  use decorating icing

1. Grease and line a deep 25 × 18 cm (10 × 7 inch) cake tin (see
page 81).
2. Preheat oven to Gas Mark 4/180°C/350°F.
3. Cream the butter and sugar together until pale and fluffy.
4. Beat in the eggs one at a time; if the mixture begins to curdle add
a tablespoon of the flour.
5. Fold in the flour and flavouring.
6. Transfer the mixture to the prepared tin. Bake just above the
centre of the oven for 30–35 minutes, until the cake is golden and
springs back when lightly pressed.
7. Turn onto a wire rack to cool, removing lining paper.
8. Use about a quarter of the sugar paste to make one small ball for
the jack, and 8 larger balls.
9. Melt the plain chocolate cake covering in a heatproof bowl
placed over a pan of hot water and use to cover 4 of the large balls.
Leave to dry. Pour the remaining covering onto a piece of
parchment paper and leave to set.
10. Coat the 4 remaining large balls with the milk chocolate
covering in the same way.
11. Brush the cake with apricot glaze and place on a board.
12. Knead some green colouring into the remaining sugar paste on
a cornfloured surface, until evenly coloured. Roll out and use to
cover the cake (see page 89).
13. Using the writing nozzle on the chocolate icing tube, pipe a
straight line along the top rim of the cake and a border along the
bottom rim. Write the teams' names on the sides.
14. Cut an oblong shape, approximately 5 × 2.5 cm (2 × 1 inch), out
of the set cake covering. Using the writing nozzle on the white icing
tube pipe a white rim around the edge. Place on the cake to
represent a mat.
15. Place the bowls and jack on the cake. Set aside to dry.

GOLF COURSE

1 cake baked as for Fondant
   Fancies (page 8), uncut
TO DECORATE:
2 quantities Butter Icing (page
   82)

few drops each Supercook
   yellow and green colouring
1 tube each Supercook blue and
   green ready to use
   decorating icing
4 Supercook silver balls

1. Place the cake on a cake board.
2. Remove approximately 50 g (2 oz) of the butter icing and colour yellow. Colour the rest green.
3. Coat the cake with the green icing, smoothing with a palette knife. Leave the centre smooth for the fairway; rough up the rest with a fork.
4. Form bunkers on the cake with the yellow icing, using a teaspoon.
5. Using the leaf nozzle on the blue icing tube, pipe on some blue lines as streams.
6. Using the writing nozzle on the green icing tube, pipe an oblong, approximately 5 × 2.5 cm (2 × 1 inch), at the beginning of the fairway to act as a mat. Pipe on the hole number, which could be the birthday number, if wished.
7. Use a cocktail stick with paper stuck on as the flag to mark the hole.
8. Place the silver balls on as golf balls.
9. Remove the flag before serving.

Illustrated below: Bowling Green

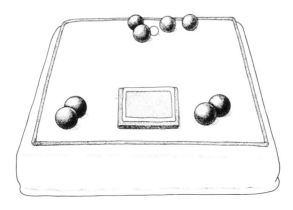

ARTIST'S EASEL

The idea of this cake is to make the easel and then let the birthday child paint on their own picture.

1 Swiss roll mixture (page 26)
2 tablespoons Apricot Glaze
  (page 86)
350 g (12 oz) drum Supercook
  ready to use fondant icing

1 tube Supercook red ready to
  use decorating icing
10 chocolate finger biscuits
1 packet Supercook decorating
  gels
1 drum Supercook sugar stars

---

1. Grease and line a 28 × 18 cm (11 × 7 inch) Swiss roll tin (see page 81).
2. Preheat oven to Gas Mark 5/190°C/375°F.
3. Transfer the Swiss roll mixture to the prepared tin and bake just above the centre of the oven for 15–20 minutes, until the cake springs back when lightly pressed.
4. Cool on a wire rack, removing lining paper.
5. Trim the edges of the cake to neaten and place the cake on a cake board. Brush with the apricot glaze.
6. Roll out the fondant and use to cover the cake (see page 89), reserving any trimmings.
7. Using the writing nozzle on the icing tube, pipe a red wavy line around the top edge of the cake.
8. Sandwich the chocolate fingers together in pairs with a little icing and arrange underneath the cake to form the easel.
9. Roll out the reserved fondant icing trimmings and cut out an artist's palette shape, if you wish.
10. Using the decorating gels, place a circle of each colour on the palette to represent paint. Place this next to the easel. Rest a Supercook birthday candle on the palette to represent a paintbrush.
11. Allow the child to draw a picture using the gels and sugar stars.

Illustrated top: Guitar (page 54); bottom: Artist's Easel

GUITAR

1 Victoria sandwich mixture
(page 22)
3 tablespoons Apricot Glaze
(page 86)
Supercook chocolate colouring
500 g (1 lb) Supercook ready to
use fondant icing

1 tube each Supercook
chocolate and white ready to
use decorating icing
6 Supercook chocolate
decorations
6 Supercook flaked almonds

1. Grease and line a 30 × 20 cm (12 × 8 inch) Swiss roll tin (see page 81).
2. Preheat oven to Gas Mark 4/180°C/350°F.
3. Transfer the cake mixture to the prepared tin. Bake just above the centre of the oven for 25–30 minutes, until the cake springs back when lightly pressed.
4. Turn onto a wire rack to cool, removing lining paper.
5. Cut the cake into a guitar shape (Fig. i) and assemble on a board.
6. Brush the cake with the apricot glaze.
7. On a surface sprinkled with cornflour, knead several drops of chocolate colouring into the fondant icing until evenly coloured. Roll out and use to cover the cake (see page 89).
8. Using the writing nozzle on the chocolate icing tube, pipe a line on the body of the guitar where the hole would be, a line at each end of the guitar to 'attach' the strings, and a row of lines for frets.
9. Using the writing nozzle on the white icing tube, pipe on the strings. Decorate the guitar with the chocolate decorations.
10. Push the almonds into the sides as the keys. Set aside to dry.

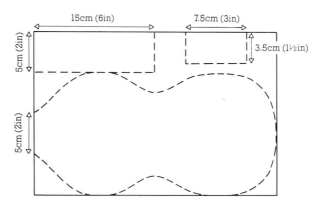

Illustrated on page 53

Fig. i

MR MEN CAR

250 g (8 oz) plain flour
2 teaspoons Supercook baking
   powder
4 large eggs, beaten
250 g (8 oz) soft margarine
250 g (8 oz) caster sugar
TO DECORATE:
100 g (3½ oz) Supercook plain
   chocolate cake covering

4 tablespoons Apricot Glaze
   (page 86)
500 g (1 lb) Supercook ready to
   use fondant icing
1 tube Supercook blue ready to
   use decorating icing
4 Supercook Mr Men edible
   wafers
1 drum Supercook sugar stars

1. Grease and line a deep 25 × 18 cm (10 × 7 inch) cake tin (see page 81). Preheat oven to Gas Mark 4/180°C/350°F.
2. Sift together the flour and baking powder. Add the remaining cake ingredients and beat until the mixture is pale and fluffy.
3. Transfer the mixture to the prepared tin. Bake just above the centre of the oven for 40–45 minutes, until the cake is golden and springs back when lightly pressed. Turn onto a wire rack to cool.
4. Cut the cake as shown in Fig. i. Position pieces A and B on a board, trimming piece A as shown in Fig. ii, for the roof.
5. Split the two 5 cm (2 inch) circles of cake in half, for 4 wheels.
6. Melt the cake covering in a heatproof bowl placed over a pan of hot water. Use to coat the 4 wheels, and leave to dry on foil.
7. Brush the cake with apricot glaze. Roll out the fondant icing and use to cover the car body (see page 89).
8. Using the blue icing with the writing tip, pipe windows onto the car, sides, back and front and place the Mr. Men wafers within. Stick sugar stars onto the car as lights.
9. When the wheels are dry, place them onto the sides of the car, securing with a little icing. Set aside to dry.

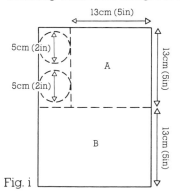

Fig. i

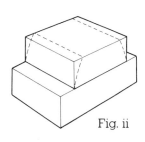

Fig. ii

'TRAIN' BIRTHDAY CAKE

150 g (5 oz) self-raising flour
25 g (1 oz) cocoa powder
1 teaspoon Supercook baking
   powder
175 g (6 oz) soft margarine
175 g (6 oz) caster sugar
3 eggs, beaten
75 g (3 oz) Supercook chocolate
   chips

TO DECORATE:
1 quantity Butter Icing (page 82)
1 Supercook birthday icing card
   with train
1 tube Supercook blue ready to
   use decorating icing

1. Grease and line a deep 25 × 18 cm (10 × 7 inch) oblong cake tin (see page 81).
2. Preheat oven to Gas Mark 4/180°C/350°F.
3. Sift the flour, cocoa powder and baking powder into a bowl.
4. Add the margarine, sugar and eggs and beat until the mixture is smooth, pale and fluffy.
5. Fold in the chocolate chips.
6. Transfer the mixture to the prepared tin. Bake just above the centre of the oven for 25–30 minutes, until the cake is golden and springs back when lightly pressed.
7. Turn onto a wire rack to cool, removing lining paper.
8. Cover the cake with the butter icing, smoothing with a palette knife. Transfer the cake to a cake board.
9. Using the icing card as instructed, arrange the pieces on the cake.
10. Using the leaf nozzle on the icing tube, pipe a border around the top edge.
11. Finish with Supercook candles in holders.

'BALLERINA' BIRTHDAY CAKE

175 g (6 oz) butter or margarine
175 g (6 oz) caster sugar
3 eggs, beaten
175 g (6 oz) self-raising flour,
   sifted
75 g (3 oz) desiccated coconut
1 tablespoon Supercook
   coconut flavouring
few drops Supercook pink
   colouring

TO FINISH:
3 tablespoons strawberry jam
2 tablespoons Apricot Glaze
   (page 86)
50 g (2 oz) Supercook sugar
   strands
1 quantity coconut Glacé Icing
   (page 82)
1 Supercook birthday icing card
   with ballerina

1. Grease and base-line two 20 cm (8 inch) sandwich tins (see page 81).

2. Preheat oven to Gas Mark 4/180°C/350°F.

3. Cream the butter or margarine and sugar together until pale and fluffy.

4. Beat in the eggs, one at a time; if the mixture begins to curdle add a tablespoon of the flour with the second egg.

5. Using a metal spoon, fold in the flour, coconut and flavouring.

6. Place half the mixture in one tin. Colour the remainder pink and place in the second tin.

7. Bake just above the centre of the oven for 20–25 minutes, until the cakes are golden and spring back when lightly pressed.

8. Turn onto a wire rack to cool, removing lining paper.

9. Sandwich the cakes together with the jam.

10. Brush the side of the cake with apricot glaze. Place the sugar strands on a plate. Roll the cake in them to coat the side. Transfer to a serving plate.

11. Cover the top of the cake with the glacé icing.

12. Using the icing card as instructed, arrange the pieces on the cake. Finish with Supercook candles in holders.

'FLOWER BASKET' BIRTHDAY CAKE

175 g (6 oz) self-raising flour
1 teaspoon Supercook baking
powder
175 g (6 oz) caster sugar
175 g (6 oz) soft margarine
3 eggs, beaten
1 tablespoon Supercook
strawberry flavouring
SUGAR PASTE:
425 g (15 oz) icing sugar, sifted
1½ tablespoons liquid glucose

1 teaspoon Supercook lemon
juice
1 teaspoon Supercook glycerine
1 small egg white
TO FINISH:
3 tablespoons Apricot Glaze
(page 86)
1 tube Supercook ready to use
white decorating icing
1 Supercook birthday icing card
with flower basket

1. Grease and line a deep 23 cm (9 inch) round cake tin (see page 81).
2. Preheat oven to Gas Mark 4/180°C/350°F.
3. Sift the flour and baking powder into a bowl.
4. Add the remaining ingredients and beat well until the mixture is smooth, pale and fluffy.
5. Transfer the mixture to the prepared tin. Bake in the centre of the oven for 45–50 minutes, until the cake is golden and springs back when lightly pressed.
6. Turn onto a wire rack to cool, removing lining paper.
7. Prepare the sugar paste as described on page 88.
8. Brush the cake with apricot glaze, then transfer to a Supercook 25 cm (10 inch) round cake board.
9. Cover the cake with the sugar paste as described on page 89.
10. Using the star nozzle on the icing tube, pipe a border around the top edge of the cake. Place a pink Supercook cake frill around the cake, securing in position with a little icing.
11. Using the icing card as instructed, place the pieces on the cake. Position Supercook candles in holders on the cake and set aside to dry.

VARIATION

To make an attractive cake for a friend or relative, use the icing card with the alphabet range. Arrange the letters and flowers on the cake, as shown on the front cover.

CELEBRATION CAKES

A beautifully iced cake makes the perfect centrepiece for any special occasion. You can easily adapt the cakes in this chapter by simply changing the colour or decoration. Instructions are given in the reference section for making a template (page 92), so you may prefer to draw your own design.

The single tier wedding cake on pages 72–3 is simple but very effective; pretty cut-out flowers and ribbon are used to maximum effect. If you are experienced you might prefer to make the attractive, though more time consuming, Tiered Rose Wedding Cake (pages 68–9). The handy reference section at the back of the book contains information on piping and royal icing and will help you produce a perfect result.

It is worth remembering that you can make the rich fruit cakes in advance – in fact they improve in flavour if made up to 3 months earlier than required. When completely cold, wrap in foil and store in a cool place.

Illustrated opposite: Engagement Cake (page 62)

ENGAGEMENT CAKE

It is advisable to pipe the bells at least a few days before the cake is required, and position them on the cake at the last moment.

20 cm (8 inch) square Rich Fruit Cake (pages 66–7)
3 tablespoons Apricot Glaze (page 86)
2 × 400 g packets Supercook marzipan
1 quantity Sugar Paste (page 88)
1 tube each Supercook white, blue and pink ready to use decorating icing
1 drum Supercook silver balls
TO FINISH:
2 metres (2 yards) 2·5 mm (⅛ inch) wide silver ribbon

1. Brush the cake with apricot glaze and cover with the marzipan (see page 86). Place the cake on a Supercook 25 cm (10 inch) board.
2. Roll out the sugar paste and use to cover the cake (see page 89). Set aside to dry.
3. Using the writing nozzle on the white icing tube, make 30 bells (see pages 84–5). (This allows 6 spare for breakages.) Leave to dry.
4. Using the writing nozzle on the white icing tube, write the man's name across one corner of the cake and the girl's name opposite. Using the writing nozzle on the pink icing tube over-pipe the girl's name. Using the writing nozzle on the blue icing tube over-pipe the man's name.
5. Make a horseshoe template (see pages 92–4) and transfer onto the top of the cake, in the centre.
6. Using the writing nozzle on the white icing tube, over-pipe the horseshoe shape. Place silver balls at intervals along the horseshoe.
7. Using the leaf nozzle on the white icing tube, pipe a border along the top and bottom edges of the cake and down each corner.
8. Attach the bells to the cake with a little white icing; 2 in each top corner; 2 on each side; 2 in each bottom corner.
9. Using the silver ribbon, make 12 tiny bows and attach to the cake beside the bells.

Makes one 20 cm (8 inch) square cake

Illustrated on page 61

EIGHTEENTH BIRTHDAY CAKE

250 g (8 oz) self-raising flour
1½ teaspoons Supercook
  baking powder
250 g (8 oz) soft margarine
250 g (8 oz) caster sugar
4 eggs, beaten
grated rind and juice of 1 lemon

TO DECORATE:
2 teaspoons Supercook lemon
  flavouring
few drops Supercook yellow
  colouring
2 quantities Butter Icing (page
  82)
2 tubes Supercook white ready
  to use decorating icing

1. Grease and base-line a 28 × 18 cm (11 × 7 inch) oblong cake tin and two 18 cm (7 inch) sandwich tins (see page 81).
2. Preheat oven to Gas Mark 4/180°C/350°F.
3. Sift the flour and baking powder into a bowl.
4. Add the remaining ingredients and beat until the mixture is pale.
5. Place half the mixture in the prepared oblong tin and divide the rest between the sandwich tins. Bake just above the centre of the oven for 20–25 minutes, until the cakes are golden and spring back when lightly pressed.
6. Turn onto a wire rack to cool, removing lining paper.
7. Shape the cakes into the number 18: remove the centres from the sandwich cakes, using a 7.5 cm (3 inch) plain cutter, to form a number 8; cut the oblong cake according to Fig. i, and arrange to form a number 1 (Fig. ii). Place the cakes on a tray or board.
8. Beat the flavouring and colouring into the butter icing. Cover the cakes with the icing, smoothing with a palette knife.
9. Using the star nozzle on the icing tube, pipe a shell border around the top and bottom edges of the cakes. Finish with Supercook candles in holders. Leave to dry.

Makes one 18-shaped cake, 36 cm (14 inch) long

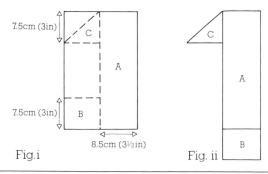

Fig.i   Fig. ii

21ST BIRTHDAY CAKE

23 cm (9 inch) round Rich Fruit
  Cake (pages 66–7)
3 tablespoons Apricot Glaze
  (page 86)
3 × 400 g packets Supercook
  marzipan

3 quantities Royal Icing (page
  90)
1 tube each Supercook white
  and blue ready to use
  decorating icing

1. Brush the cake with apricot glaze and cover with the marzipan (pages 86–7). Place on a Supercook 25 cm (10 inch) round board.
2. Use the royal icing to coat the cake (pages 90–1). Apply 2 coats.
3. Make templates for the figure 21 and a scroll and transfer onto the top of the cake (see pages 92–4). Using the writing nozzle on the white icing tube, pipe a double line over the 21 and 4 scrolls.
4. Using the writing nozzle on the blue icing tube, over-pipe a double line over the 21 and 4 scrolls. Leave to set.
5. Using the writing nozzle on the white icing tube, pipe a line on top of the blue 21. Change to the star nozzle and pipe stars around the top and bottom edges. Leave to dry.
6. To finish, secure a Supercook blue cake frill around the cake or blue and white ribbons.

VARIATION
To make a pretty pink and white 21st birthday cake, coat the cake with white royal icing. Tint any left over royal icing pink, using Supercook colouring, and place in a nylon piping bag, fitted with a ribbon nozzle. Use to make about 15 flowers (see pages 84–5)—this includes 3 spare to allow for breakages. Using Supercook pink ready to use decorating icing, instead of blue, pipe the figure 21, as described above. Make a template for a key (see pages 92–4) and transfer onto the top of the cake instead of the scrolls. Pipe a double pink line over the key shape, then pipe a white line on top. Using the leaf nozzle on the pink icing tube, pipe a border around the top and bottom edges of the cake. Secure 3 flowers in each corner with a little icing. Finish with a Supercook pink cake frill.

Makes one 23 cm (9 inch) round cake

RICH FRUIT CAKE

Use this chart as your ingredients list for the 21st Birthday, Engagement and Wedding Cakes, following the appropriate size column. Make the cakes as instructed below and cook for the time given at the end of the columns; start with the higher temperature then lower heat.

1. Prepare the cake tins (see page 81) and preheat oven to the temperature specified below.
2. Sift together the flour, cinnamon and mixed spice.
3. Cream the butter and sugar together in a large mixing bowl until pale and fluffy.

RICH FRUIT CAKE QUANTITIES AND COOKING TIMES		
	15 cm (6 inch) square	20 cm (8 inch) square
Plain flour	175 g (6 oz)	375 g (13 oz)
Ground cinnamon	½ teaspoon	1 teaspoon
Ground mixed spice	½ teaspoon	1 teaspoon
Butter, softened	175 g (6 oz)	300 g (10 oz)
Soft dark brown sugar	175 g (6 oz)	300 g (10 oz)
Large eggs, beaten	3	5
Grated lemon rind	½ lemon	1 lemon
Cleaned currants	300 g (10 oz)	575 g (1 lb 3 oz)
Cleaned sultanas	125 g (4 oz)	250 g (8 oz)
Cleaned raisins	125 g (4 oz)	200 g (7 oz)
Glacé cherries, quartered, rinsed and dried	75 g (3 oz)	150 g (5 oz)
Chopped mixed peel	50 g (2 oz)	100 g (3½ oz)
Supercook flaked almonds	50 g (2 oz)	100 g (3½ oz)
Brandy or sherry (optional)	2 tablespoons	2 tablespoons
Gas Mark 2/150°C/300°F	1 hour	2 hours
Gas Mark 1/140°C/275°F	2½–3 hours	1–1½ hour

4. Beat in the eggs a little at a time; if the mixture begins to curdle add a tablespoon of the flour mixture after each 2 eggs.
5. Fold in the flour mixture, then stir in the remaining ingredients, except the brandy or sherry.
6. Transfer the mixture to the tin and make a slight hollow in the centre. Bake in the centre of the oven (below centre for the 30 cm (12 inch) round cake) as instructed below, until a skewer pierced through the centre of the cake comes out clean. If the top starts to brown too much, cover with a layer of greaseproof paper.
7. Remove from the oven and leave to stand for 30 minutes. Turn onto a wire rack to cool, removing lining paper.
8. If wished, pierce holes in the base of the cake with a skewer and spoon in the brandy or sherry. Wrap the cake in foil to store.

23 cm (9 inch) round	25 cm (10 inch) square	30 cm (12 inch) round
525 g (1 lb 1 oz)	675 g (1 lb 6 oz)	1 kg (2 lb)
1½ teaspoons	2 teaspoons	3 teaspoons
1 teaspoon	1½ teaspoons	2 teaspoons
425 g (15 oz)	575 g (1 lb 3 oz)	900 g (1 lb 14 oz)
425 g (15 oz)	575 g (1 lb 3 oz)	900 g (1 lb 14 oz)
8	10	15
1 lemon	1 lemon	2 lemons
750 g (1½ lb)	500 g (1 lb)	1.5 kg (3 lb)
300 g (10 oz)	500 g (1 lb)	500 g (1 lb)
300 g (10 oz)	500 g (1 lb)	500 g (1 lb)
250 g (8 oz)	250 g (8 oz)	350 g (12 oz)
125 g (4 oz)	150 g (5 oz)	300 g (10 oz)
125 g (4 oz)	125 g (4 oz)	275 g (9 oz)
3 tablespoons	3 tablespoons	4 tablespoons
2 hours	3 hours	4 hours
2½–3 hours	2–2½ hours	3½–4 hours

TIERED ROSE WEDDING CAKE

1 each 15, 20 and 25 cm (6, 8 and
   10 inch) square Rich Fruit
   Cakes (pages 66–7)
6 tablespoons Apricot Glaze
   (page 86)
6 × 400 g packets Supercook
   marzipan

TO COAT:
3 × 3 quantities Royal Icing,
   without glycerine (page 90)
TO DECORATE:
5 quantities Royal Icing, without
   glycerine (page 90)
few drops each Supercook pink
   and green colouring

1. Brush the cakes with apricot glaze, then cover with the marzipan (see pages 86–7). Place the cakes on boards.

2. Making 3 quantities of royal icing at a time, apply 1 coat of royal icing to the cakes (see pages 90–1). Apply 2 more coats of royal icing to each cake in the same way.

3. To decorate, tint 1 quantity of the royal icing with a few drops of pink food colouring. Place in a greaseproof or nylon piping bag, fitted with a petal nozzle, and use to make 60 roses (see pages 84–5)—this will allow 12 spare for breakages.

4. Lightly mark with a pin the centre point of each top edge on the cakes. Mark the top edges of the cakes into 1 cm (½ inch) sections.

5. Half-fill a greaseproof or nylon piping bag, fitted with a No. 2 writing nozzle, with the royal icing. Use to pipe a lattice in each corner of the cakes as instructed on page 83.

6. Using a star nozzle, pipe rows of stars at an angle along the top edges of the cakes with the white royal icing. Pipe rows of stars around the bottom edges of the cakes and down each side at the corners.

7. Make loop templates and transfer to the sides of the cakes (see page 92). Using the greaseproof or nylon piping bag, fitted with a No. 2 writing nozzle, pipe over the marked loops on the sides of the cakes.

8. Tint the remaining royal icing with a few drops of green food colouring. Place in a greaseproof or nylon piping bag fitted with a leaf nozzle. Pipe 3 leaves at each centre point on the top edges of the cakes; 3 on each side of the cakes where the loops join at the top and 3 below each loop.

9. Place one rose in between each group of leaves.

10. To finish, assemble the tiers using 8 square cake pillars and arrange a spray of flowers on the top.

Makes one 3-tiered cake

VALENTINE CAKE

150 g (5 oz) self-raising flour
25 g (1 oz) cocoa powder
175 g (6 oz) butter or margarine
175 g (6 oz) caster sugar
3 eggs, beaten
175 g (6 oz) glacé cherries,
   quartered, rinsed and dried

TO DECORATE:
3 tablespoons Apricot Glaze
   (page 86)
1 quantity Sugar Paste (page 88)
1 tube Supercook red ready to
   use decorating icing

1. Grease and line a deep 20 cm (8 inch) heart-shaped tin (see page 81).
2. Preheat oven to Gas Mark 4/180°C/350°F.
3. Sift together the flour and cocoa powder.
4. Cream the butter or margarine and sugar together until pale and fluffy.
5. Beat in the eggs, one at a time; if the mixture begins to curdle add a tablespoon of the flour after the second egg.
6. Fold in the flour and cherries.
7. Transfer the mixture to the prepared tin. Bake just above the centre of the oven for 50–55 minutes, until the cake is golden and springs back when lightly pressed.
8. Turn onto a wire rack to cool, removing lining paper.
9. Brush the cake with the apricot glaze, then roll out the sugar paste and use to cover the cake (see page 89). Set aside to dry.
10. Using the petal nozzle on the icing tube, pipe 12–15 roses (see pages 84–5). Leave to dry.
11. Using the writing nozzle, write the words 'Be Mine' on the cake. Pipe a single line around the top edge and a border of dots around the bottom edge.
12. Arrange the roses in a heart shape on top of the cake.

VARIATION
Instead of piping roses and a message on the cake, you could use the Supercook pink alphabet icing card—simply arrange the flowers and letters on top of the cake as instructed. You may also wish to pipe around the top and bottom edges of the cake using a tube of Supercook pink ready to use decorating icing, in place of the red icing.

Makes one 20 cm (8 inch) cake

GOLDEN WEDDING ANNIVERSARY CAKE

250 g (8 oz) plain flour
50 g (2 oz) self-raising flour
2 teaspoons ground mixed
  spice
250 g (8 oz) butter, softened
250 g (8 oz) soft dark brown
  sugar
4 large eggs, beaten
250 g (8 oz) cleaned sultanas
250 g (8 oz) cleaned raisins
125 g (4 oz) glacé cherries,
  quartered, rinsed and dried
175 g (6 oz) chopped mixed
  peel
50 g (2 oz) Supercook flaked
  almonds

2–3 tablespoons brandy or
  sherry (optional)
TO DECORATE:
3 tablespoons Apricot Glaze
  (page 86)
2 × 400 g packets Supercook
  marzipan
3 quantities Royal Icing (page
  90)
1 Supercook anniversary icing
  card with yellow figures
2 tubes Supercook white ready
  to use decorating icing
1 drum Supercook silver balls

1. Prepare a deep 30 cm (12 inch) horseshoe cake tin, placed on a baking tray (see page 81).
2. Preheat oven to Gas Mark 2/150°C/300°F.
3. Make the cake as instructed on pages 66–7.
4. Transfer the mixture to the tin and make a slight hollow in the top. Bake in the centre of the oven for 1½ hours. Lower the temperature to Gas Mark 1/140°C/275°F and bake for another 1½ hours, until a skewer pierced through the centre comes out clean.
5. Turn onto a wire rack to cool, removing lining paper.
6. If wished, pierce several holes in the base of the cake with a skewer and spoon in the brandy or sherry. Wrap the cake in foil and store for up to three months.
7. Brush the cake with apricot glaze, then cover the cake with marzipan (see pages 86–7). Cover with 2–3 coats of royal icing as for a round cake (see pages 90–1).
8. Using the icing card as instructed, arrange the words 'Happy 50th Anniversary' along the cake and the decorations at either end.
9. Using the star nozzle on the icing tube, pipe fancy scrolls around the top edge; finish each with a silver ball. Pipe a shell border around the bottom edge.
10. Finish with a wide golden ribbon around the outside edge, securing with icing.

Makes one 30 cm (12 inch) horseshoe cake

SIMPLE WEDDING CAKE

Placing the ribbon on the cake is really quite easy, but does require patience. If you prefer, simply tie a ribbon around the cake.

30 cm (12 inch) round Rich Fruit Cake (pages 66–7)
3–4 tablespoons Apricot Glaze (page 86)
4 × 400 g packets Supercook marzipan

3 quantities Sugar Paste (page 88)
few drops Supercook yellow colouring
TO FINISH:
2 metres (2 yards) 5 mm (¼ inch) wide white ribbon

1. Brush the cake with apricot glaze and cover with the marzipan (see page 86).
2. Set aside 125 g (4 oz) of the sugar paste—colour the rest yellow, roll out and use to cover the cake (see page 89).
3. Cut the ribbon into twenty-six 3 cm (1¼ inch) lengths.
4. Using a sharp pointed knife, make vertical 1 cm (½ inch) slits through the icing (without cutting the marzipan) at 2.5 cm (1 inch) intervals all the way around the side of the cake. Make another row of slits 1 cm (½ inch) above the first row.
5. Carefully push the pieces of ribbon into the slits. Push each slit closed, using fingers dipped in cornflour, so that the ribbon is held in place. Repeat on the second row.
6. Make 2 bows with the remaining ribbon and attach to the cake.
7. Roll out the reserved white sugar paste and cut out approximately 55 small flowers, and 30 large flowers using flower cutters.
8. Using icing or egg white, stick the small flowers on the cake between the ribbons. Stick the larger flowers around the top edge.
9. Arrange the remaining cut-out flowers in the centre of the cake; alternatively place a spray of flowers or sugar-frosted flowers (see below) on top of the cake.

TO MAKE SUGAR-FROSTED FLOWERS
Simple flowers are most successful for this treatment. For this cake select several fresh, dry primroses. Using a small paintbrush, coat each flower all over with lightly beaten egg white. Carefully spoon over caster sugar to coat the flowers evenly. Place on a wire rack covered with a layer of kitchen paper. Set aside in a warm dry place until the flowers are dry and hard.

Makes one 30 cm (12 inch) round cake

HARVEST FRUIT CAKE

250 g (8 oz) plain flour
1 teaspoon ground cinnamon
1 teaspoon ground nutmeg
175 g (6 oz) butter, softened
175 g (6 oz) light brown sugar
3 eggs, beaten
350 g (12 oz) cleaned currants
125 g (4 oz) cleaned sultanas
75 g (3 oz) chopped mixed peel
400 g packet Supercook
   marzipan

few drops Supercook yellow
   colouring (optional)
1 tablespoon Apricot Glaze
   (page 86)
1 tube Supercook white ready
   to use decorating icing
1 drum Supercook marzipan
   fruits

1. Prepare a deep 18 cm (7 inch) round cake tin (see page 81).
2. Preheat oven to Gas Mark 3/170°C/325°F.
3. Sift together the flour, cinnamon and nutmeg.
4. Cream the butter and sugar together until pale and fluffy.
5. Beat in the eggs, one at a time; if the mixture begins to curdle, add a tablespoon of the flour.
6. Fold in the flour, fruit and peel.
7. Roll out half the marzipan on a sugared surface and shape to a round the same size as the tin.
8. Place half the cake mixture in the prepared tin. Lay the marzipan on top. Cover with the remaining cake mixture, smoothing the top and making a slight hollow in the centre.
9. Bake in the centre of the oven for 1 hour. Lower the temperature to Gas Mark 2/150°C/300°F and bake for another 2 hours.
10. Turn onto a wire rack to cool, then remove the lining paper.
11. Knead the colouring, if using, into the remaining marzipan, then roll out and shape into an 18 cm (7 inch) round. Brush the top of the cake with the apricot glaze and place the marzipan on top.
12. Using the decorating icing tube fitted with the writing nozzle, pipe a basket shape in the centre of the cake. Arrange the marzipan fruits as if they are in the basket.
13. Pipe a border around the edge using the leaf nozzle.
14. Tie a wide yellow ribbon around the cake to serve.

VARIATION

To make a Simnel Cake, follow steps 1–11 above. Replace the decorating icing and marzipan fruits with a 400 g packet Supercook marzipan. Form the marzipan into 13 balls, and attach 11 balls at equal intervals around the top edge of the cake, securing with a little apricot glaze. Cover the centre of the cake with foil, then place the cake under a moderate grill until the balls are brown. Shape a chick, using the 2 remaining marzipan balls; attach 2 Supercook orange jelly diamonds for a beak and 2 Supercook silver balls for eyes. Mark on wings with a knife and position the chick in the contre of the cake.

Makes one 18 cm (7 inch) cake

CHRISTMAS CAKE

Use the following recipe to make the Christmas cakes overleaf. Separate instructions are given for decorating.

250 g (8 oz) plain flour
50 g (2 oz) self-raising flour
2 teaspoons ground mixed
  spice
250 g (8 oz) butter, softened
250 g (8 oz) soft dark brown
  sugar
4 eggs, beaten
250 g (8 oz) cleaned currants
250 g (8 oz) cleaned raisins

125 g (4 oz) glacé cherries,
  quartered, rinsed and dried
175 g (6 oz) chopped mixed
  peel
50 g (2 oz) Supercook flaked
  almonds
2 tablespoons Apricot Glaze
  (page 86)
2 × 400 g packets Supercook
  marzipan

1. Prepare a 20 cm (8 inch) round or square cake tin (see page 81).
2. Preheat oven to Gas Mark 2/150°C/300°F.
3. Sift the flours and mixed spice together.
4. Cream the butter and sugar together in a large mixing bowl until pale and fluffy.
5. Beat in the eggs a little at a time; if the mixture begins to curdle add a tablespoon of the flour with the third egg.
6. Fold in the flour, then stir in the remaining ingredients.
7. Transfer the mixture to the prepared tin and make a slight hollow in the centre. Bake in the centre of the oven for 1 hour, then lower the temperature to Gas Mark 1/140°C/275°F and bake for another 3 hours for the square cake, 3½ hours for the round cake, or until a skewer pierced through the centre of the cake comes out clean.
8. Turn onto a wire rack to cool, removing lining paper.
9. Brush the cake with the apricot glaze, then cover with the marzipan (see pages 86–7).

Makes one 20 cm (8 inch) cake

SIMPLE CHRISTMAS CAKE

20 cm (8 inch) round
   marzipanned cake (page 75)
1 quantity Royal Icing (page 90)

1 Supercook Christmas Icing
   card

1. Cover the cake with the royal icing, spreading it all over. Rough up the side and a border around the top of the cake with a knife.
2. Using the icing card as instructed, arrange the pieces on the cake.
3. Finish with a Supercook cake frill.

Makes one 20 cm (8 inch) round cake

HOLLY LEAF CHRISTMAS CAKE

20 cm (8 inch) square
   marzipanned cake (page 75)
2 quantities Royal Icing (page 90)
200 g packet Supercook marzipan

few drops Supercook cochineal
few drops Supercook green colouring
1 tube each red and white Supercook ready to use decorating icing

1. Cover the cake with 2 coats of royal icing (see pages 90–1).
2. Take 25 g (1 oz) of the marzipan and colour it red with the cochineal. Roll into 15 tiny balls to form holly berries.
3. Colour the remaining marzipan green, roll out and cut into 11 holly leaves.
4. Using the leaf nozzle on the white icing tube, pipe a border around the top and bottom edges and down each corner of the cake.
5. Using the writing nozzle on the red icing tube, pipe dots along the white border.
6. Arrange 2 holly leaves and 3 berries in each corner of the cake and 3 leaves and 3 berries in the centre of the cake.

Makes one 20 cm (8 inch) square cake

STAR CHRISTMAS CAKE

This cake—and the Christening Cake opposite—have been included for those who prefer a lighter fruit cake.

175 g (6 oz) self raising flour
½ teaspoon ground cinnamon
1 teaspoon ground mixed spice
175 g (6 oz) butter, softened
175 g (6 oz) light brown sugar
3 large eggs, beaten
75 g (3 oz) Supercook chopped walnuts
375 g (13 oz) cleaned mixed dried fruit

TO DECORATE:
2 tablespoons Apricot Glaze (page 86)
2 × 400 g packets Supercook marzipan
1 quantity Sugar Paste (page 88)
1 tube each Supercook white and red ready to use decorating icing

1. Prepare a 20 cm (8 inch) round cake tin (see page 81).
2. Preheat oven to Gas Mark 3/170°C/325°F.
3. Sift together the flour, cinnamon and mixed spice.
4. Cream the butter and sugar together in a mixing bowl until pale and fluffy.
5. Beat in the eggs a little at a time; if the mixture begins to curdle, add a tablespoon of the flour mixture.
6. Fold in the flour mixture, then stir in the remaining ingredients.
7. Transfer the mixture to the prepared tin and make a slight hollow in the centre. Bake for 1½ hours then lower the heat to Gas Mark 2/150°C/300°F and bake for another 40 minutes or until a skewer pierced through the cake comes out clean.
8. Remove from the oven and leave the cake in the tin for 10 minutes. Turn onto a wire rack to cool, removing lining paper.
9. To decorate, brush with the apricot glaze then cover with the marzipan (see page 86).
10. Cover the cake with the sugar paste (see page 89).
11. Make a star template as described on page 92 and transfer the pattern to the top of the cake.
12. Using the writing nozzle on the white icing tube outline the star onto the top of the cake. Pipe lines parallel to the sides of the star to fill in the outer areas.
13. Using the writing nozzle on the red icing tube, write 'Happy Christmas' in the centre of the star.
14. Tie a red ribbon around the outside of the cake.
15. To finish, using the star nozzle on the white icing tube pipe a border of stars around the bottom edge.

CHRISTENING CAKE

200 g (7 oz) self raising flour
½ teaspoon ground nutmeg
½ teaspoon ground cinnamon
175 g (6 oz) butter, softened
175 g (6 oz) soft dark brown
  sugar
4 large eggs, beaten
75 g (3 oz) glace cherries,
  quartered, rinsed and dried
50 g (2 oz) ground almonds
350 g (12 oz) cleaned mixed
  dried fruit

TO DECORATE:
2 tablespoons Apricot Glaze
  (page 80)
2 × 400 g packets Supercook
  marzipan
1 quantity Sugar Paste (page 88)
few drops Supercook pink or
  blue colouring
1 tube Supercook pink or blue
  ready to use decorating
  icing

1. Prepare a 20 cm (8 inch) square cake tin (see page 81).
2. Preheat oven to Gas Mark 3/170°C/325°F.
3. Sift together the flour, nutmeg and cinnamon.
4. Cream the butter and sugar together in a mixing bowl until pale.
5. Beat in the eggs a little at a time; if the mixture begins to curdle, add a tablespoon of the flour mixture. Fold in the flour mixture, then stir in the remaining ingredients.
6. Transfer the mixture to the prepared tin and make a slight hollow in the centre.
7. Bake for 1½ hours then lower the oven temperature to Gas Mark 2/150°C/300°F and bake for another 20 minutes, or until a skewer pierced through the centre of the cake comes out clean.
8. Remove from the oven and leave the cake in the tin for 10 minutes. Turn onto a wire rack, removing the lining paper.
9. To decorate, brush with the apricot glaze and then cover with the marzipan (see page 86).
10. Set aside approximately 100 g (3½ oz) of sugar paste. Cover the cake with the remaining sugar paste (see page 89).
11. Using the colouring, tint the reserved sugar paste either pink or blue. Make two bootees: Roll the sugar paste into two short fat sausage shapes, then bend one end round to form the toe of each booty. Using a cocktail stick, hollow out the other end and draw a pattern on each. Tie a thin piece of ribbon around the top edge of each booty and make a bow.
12. Using the pink or blue icing tube with the writing nozzle, write the baby's name on the cake and place the bootees in position.
13. Tie either pink or blue thick ribbon around the cake, and make 4 bows from thin ribbon, attaching one to each corner.
14. To finish, using the writing nozzle on the pink or blue icing tube, pipe a wavy line around the bottom edge of the cake.

REFERENCE SECTION

As well as basic recipes for icings, included here are useful instructions for lining cake tins, piping a variety of designs, applying marzipan and royal icing, and making templates. With the help of step-by-step diagrams, you will be able to achieve perfect results every time.

EQUIPMENT

In addition to basic cake-making equipment such as a wooden spoon, accurate weighing scales, set of measuring spoons, scissors, pencil, spatula, sieve, whisk and measuring jug, the following items will come in handy for cake icing and decorating.

Palette knife: for smoothing icings such as butter icing.
Greaseproof paper: for lining tins.
Cutters: round, plain and fluted cutters of various sizes are useful when making small cakes. Flower cutters are very useful for making attractive decorations from sugar paste or marzipan. Cutters for leaves, holly leaves, numbers and letters are also available—handy when you are in a hurry.
Brushes: it is useful to have quite a large brush for applying apricot glaze, a medium-size brush for greasing cake tins, and a small brush for applying details to novelty cakes.
Piping bags: nylon piping bags are useful for piping cream and other icings. They come in various sizes. For piping royal icing, greaseproof paper piping bags are more suitable.
Nozzles: Supercook ready to use icings come complete with 4 screw on nozzles: writing nozzle, leaf nozzle, star nozzle and ribbon nozzle. A selection of metal nozzles is very useful. For piping lines of royal icing a No. 2 writing nozzle has been used in this book. A range of star nozzles—of different sizes and with a variety of points—are the most versatile. Use the smaller star nozzles for royal icing and larger ones for piping cream and butter icing. For making royal icing flowers, a petal nozzle is necessary.
Scrapers: to flat ice a fruit cake using royal icing, an icing ruler and a side scraper will be invaluable to obtaining a smooth result.
Tins: start off with 18 cm (7 inch) and 20 cm (8 inch) round and square cake tins and sandwich tins. A Swiss roll tin, 28 × 18 cm (11 × 7 inch) and a deep 25 × 18 cm (10 × 7 inch) oblong cake tin are also very useful.
Turntable: although expensive this is invaluable when decorating cakes.
Flower nails: a real asset when piping roses.

PREPARATION OF CAKE TINS

Unless you use a non-stick cake tin, you will need to grease, or grease and line the tin with greaseproof paper, then grease the paper. Brush the tin with oil or melted fat, using a pastry brush or kitchen paper.

For cakes that are not to be cooked a long time e.g. Victoria sandwich or whisked sponge mixtures, dredge the greased paper with flour, shaking out any excess.

To base-line cake tins: e.g. sandwich tins (round or square)
Cut out a single layer of greaseproof paper to fit the base of the tin. Grease the paper.

To line rectangular or square tins e.g. Swiss roll, loaf tin
Use a piece of greaseproof paper large enough to stand approximately 5 cm (2 inches) higher than the tin at the sides. Place the tin upside down on the paper and cut from each corner of the paper to each corner of the tin. Fit the paper into the greased tin neatly; trim away any excess overlapping paper. Grease the paper.

To line round or square deep tins
For deep sponge cakes e.g. Victoria sandwich or whisked sponge mixtures, simply cut a single layer of greaseproof paper to fit the base and a strip to fit the side(s) of the cake tin. Fit the paper into the greased tin, then grease the paper.

As many deep cakes need longer cooking i.e. fruit cakes, the outside of the cake needs to be protected from drying and over-browning: cut a double thickness strip of greaseproof paper long enough to go round the whole tin with a small overlap and deep enough to stand approximately 5 cm (2 inches) above the top of the tin. Fold over 2.5 cm (1 inch), creasing well, and make 1 cm (½ inch) cuts at approximately 1 cm (½ inch) intervals. Position around the greased side(s) of the tin with the cut edge along the base. Grease the cut edge. Place the cake tin on a double thickness of greaseproof paper, mark and cut out round the base. Place on the greased base of the tin, over the cut edge. Grease all the lining paper.

NOTE: For rich fruit cakes requiring a long cooking time, extra protection is required: for cakes up to, and including, 20 cm (8 inches) in diameter, wrap 2 layers of brown paper around the side(s) and base of the tin before baking; for larger cakes wrap 4 layers of brown paper around the outside of the tin. Place the tin on a baking tray.

BASIC ICINGS

These quick and easy icings can transform a plain sponge into something special.

GLACÉ ICING

2 tablespoons warm water
250 g (8 oz) icing sugar, sifted

few drops Supercook colouring
(optional)

1. Gradually mix the water into the icing sugar.
2. Add colouring if wished and stir until evenly coloured.
3. Use the icing immediately.

VARIATIONS

Coconut/Butterscotch: Replace 1 tablespoon water with
1 tablespoon coconut or butterscotch flavouring.
Lemon/Coffee: Replace 2 teaspoons water with 2 teaspoons lemon or coffee flavouring.

Makes a 250 g (8 oz) quantity

BUTTER ICING

125 g (4 oz) butter, softened
250 g (8 oz) icing sugar, sifted
2 teaspoons milk

¼ teaspoon Supercook vanilla
flavouring
few drops Supercook colouring
(optional)

1. Beat the butter, then gradually add half the icing sugar.
2. Beat in the milk and flavouring. Beat in the remaining icing sugar.
3. Beat in colouring if wished.

VARIATIONS

Coffee/Butterscotch: Replace the vanilla flavouring and half the milk with 1 tablespoon coffee or butterscotch flavouring.
Brandy: Replace the vanilla flavouring and half the milk with 2 teaspoons brandy flavouring.

Makes a 250 g (8 oz) quantity

PIPING TECHNIQUES

When using a greaseproof paper or nylon piping bag, only half-fill with the icing, to make it easier to manage.

Glacé icing can be piped in lines and used to achieve the feather icing effect (below). Butter icing and whipped cream are best piped with a large star nozzle. Royal icing is ideal for piping lattice (below), straight lines, loops, and roses (see pages 84–5).

FEATHER ICING

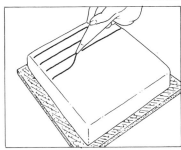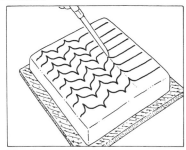

Fig. i   Fig. ii

As soon as the glacé icing is applied to the cake, pipe parallel lines of contrasting colour icing at 2.5 cm (1 inch) intervals across the cake (Fig. i). Quickly draw the point of a knife across the cake alternately in opposite directions at equal intervals perpendicular to the piped lines (Fig. ii).

LATTICE ICING

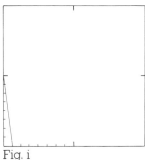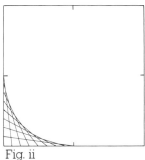

Fig. i   Fig. ii

Using a pin, lightly mark each top edge of the cake in half, then into 1 cm (½ inch) sections. Working on one corner of the cake at a time, pipe a line from the mid point of one side to the first marked point (from the corner) on the adjacent side (Fig. i). Repeat to join up the marked points (Fig. ii).

Using a ribbon (or petal) nozzle (illustrated top left)
Flowers: Work onto waxed paper or the cake. Keeping the nozzle flat, and with the thicker edge to the centre, pipe 4–5 petals, starting under the previous one each time. Leave to dry.
Roses: Using a little icing, stick a small square of waxed paper onto an icing nail. Holding the tube or bag so that the thin end of the nozzle is uppermost, pipe a cone of icing, twisting the nail between finger and thumb. Pipe 3–5 overlapping petals around the edge in the same way. Leave to dry.

Using a star nozzle (illustrated middle left)
Star: Squeeze the icing out, making a quick down and up movement.
Rosette: Squeeze the icing out in a circular movement, finishing off sharply in the centre.
Shell: Holding the tube or bag at an angle, squeeze the icing out until a head is formed. Gently pull back, releasing the pressure, to form a point. Repeat to make a border.
Scroll: Holding the tube or bag at an angle, squeeze the icing out into a comma shape, beginning with a thick head and gradually releasing the pressure to form a point. Repeat to make a border.
'S'-shaped scroll: Holding the tube or bag at an angle, squeeze the icing out into an 'S' shape. Repeat to make a border.

Using a leaf nozzle (illustrated bottom)
Lines: Holding the tube or bag at an angle, squeeze out enough icing to touch the surface, then gently squeeze, and lift the nozzle just above the surface, pulling it towards you. Touch the surface with the nozzle to break the line.
Wavy line: Holding the tube or bag at an angle move the nozzle to and fro in a wave shape, trying not to break the flow of the icing.
Leaves: Holding the tube or bag at an angle, squeeze the icing out by lifting the nozzle up and down. Apply continuous pressure to achieve a border effect or pull away sharply to give a leaf shape.

Using a writing nozzle (illustrated right, from top to bottom)
Writing: Draw the letters onto greaseproof paper. Using a pin transfer the letters onto the surface of the cake and pipe on top.
Bells: Pipe quite a large, flat, dot onto waxed paper then pipe 2 or 3 progressively smaller dots on top. Leave to dry until the outside is firm. Remove from the paper and push in a Supercook silver ball.
Dots: Squeeze the icing to make a dot of the required size, then make a quick upward movement to release the flow of icing.
Loops: Holding the nozzle away from the surface, move to allow the icing to fall in an even loop. Touch the surface to finish the loop.

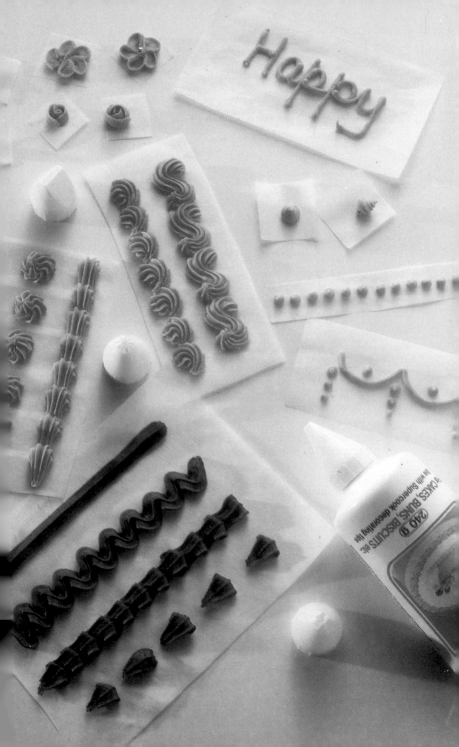

APRICOT GLAZE

This glaze is used to brush over a cake, before applying marzipan, sugar paste or fondant icing. It can also be used to attach a coating of Supercook chopped mixed nuts, chocolate flakes or chocolate sugar strands to the side(s) of a cake.

2 tablespoons apricot jam
1 teaspoon water

1. Place the jam and water in a small pan and heat gently until combined.
2. Sieve to remove any lumps, then warm up again to use.
3. Apply the apricot glaze with a brush.
4. Store any left over in a screw-top jar in the refrigerator.

Makes 2 tablespoons

NOTE: Increase or decrease the ingredients in proportion where a recipe calls for more or less apricot glaze. For instance, where a recipe states 3 tablespoons apricot glaze, use 3 tablespoons apricot jam and 1½ teaspoons water; for 1 tablespoon apricot glaze, use 1 tablespoon apricot jam and ½ teaspoon water.

TO COVER A CAKE WITH MARZIPAN
Apricot glaze (above) should be brushed over the cake before applying the marzipan.

Marzipan is used to give a smooth finish to fruit cakes which are to be covered with sugar paste or royal icing. It also prevents moisture from the cake discolouring the icing. Once the cake is covered with marzipan, leave to dry at room temperature for about 7 days before applying icing.

So that the cake has a flat top, turn it upside down onto a cake board. If there are gaps between the edge of the cake and the board fill them in with small pieces of marzipan. Use a palette knife to achieve a smooth edge.

To marzipan a cake to be covered with sugar paste: Brush the cake with Apricot Glaze (above). Roll out the marzipan on a sugared surface to a round or square large enough to cover the whole cake. Lift the marzipan onto the cake and mould it over the cake; on a square cake, cut the marzipan to fit. Trim off any excess marzipan at the bottom of the cake.

To marzipan a cake ready for royal icing

Brush the cake with Apricot Glaze (opposite). To cover the top of a round or square cake, roll out half the marzipan on a sugared surface to a round or square the same size as the top of the cake. Lift the marzipan onto the cake, trimming off any excess at the edges.

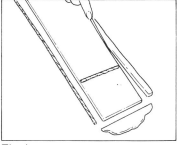

Fig. i

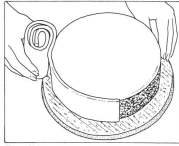

Fig. ii

To cover the side of a round cake, cut a piece of string the length of the circumference of the cake and another piece as long as the cake is deep. Roll out the remaining marzipan into a strip long enough to go round the cake, using the pieces of string as your guide (Fig. i). Neaten the edges and roll up loosely. Unroll as you attach it to the cake, pressing on gently (Fig. ii). Smooth the ends together with a small palette knife.

To cover the sides of a square cake, roll out the remaining marzipan and cut into 4 strips the same size as the sides of the cake. Press them gently onto the cake and smooth the joins together with a small palette knife.

MARZIPAN DECORATIONS

If you have any leftover marzipan you may like to mould or cut it into animals or other novelty shapes to give as presents or to decorate the finished, iced cake. Firstly, tint the marzipan by kneading in a few drops of Supercook colouring on a sugared surface, until evenly coloured. Pages 74–5 tell you how to make a chick. To make cut-out marzipan decorations, roll out the marzipan on a sugared surface then cut out the required design using a knife, cutter, or a template (see page 95).

SUGAR PASTE

500 g (1 lb) icing sugar, sifted
3 tablespoons liquid glucose
3 teaspoons Supercook lemon
  juice

1 teaspoon Supercook glycerine
1 egg white
few drops Supercook colouring
  (optional)

1. Make a well in the centre of the icing sugar.
2. Add the remaining ingredients and mix well.
3. Turn onto a cornfloured surface and knead until smooth. Add any colouring (if using) and knead until evenly coloured.
4. Wrap in clingfilm and keep in a plastic bag until required.

Makes a 500 g (1 lb) quantity

FONDANT ICING

Instead of using the Supercook ready to use fondant icing (opposite), you may prefer to make this *pouring* fondant icing. A thermometer is necessary to prepare it successfully.

150 ml (¼ pint) water
500 g (1 lb) granulated sugar

¼ teaspoon Supercook cream of
  tartar
few drops Supercook colouring
  (optional)

1. Place the water in a heavy-based pan. Add the sugar and heat gently, without stirring, until the sugar has dissolved.
2. Bring slowly to the boil, add the cream of tartar and continue to boil until 115°C/240°F is reached on the thermometer.
3. Remove from the heat, cool slightly, then carefully pour into a heatproof bowl. Leave to cool until a skin forms.
4. Using a wooden spoon, working from the outside inwards, beat well until the mixture stiffens and turns white. Knead until smooth.
5. To use, place in a heatproof bowl and heat over a pan of hot water until the consistency resembles cream; add a little water if necessary and any colouring or flavouring.
6. Pour the icing onto the cake. Smooth over with a palette knife dipped in water.

Makes a 500 g (1 lb) quantity, enough to cover a 20 cm (8 inch) cake or 8 small cakes.

FONDANT ICING

Supercook ready to use fondant icing is available in handy 350 g (12 oz) drums. Any left over will keep for at least a month in the refrigerator, if sealed in clingfilm or polythono. If tho icing appears dry after storage, knead in a few drops of water.

TO COVER A CAKE WITH SUGAR PASTE OR FONDANT ICING

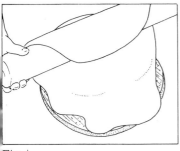

Fig. i

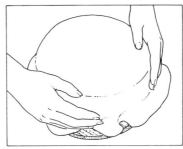

Fig. ii

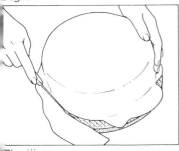

Fig. iii

Fig. iv

1. Roll out the sugar paste or fondant icing on a surface sprinkled with cornflour until 2.5–5 mm (⅛–¼ inch) thick, and large enough to cover the cake.
2. Cover the rolling pin with cornflour and use to lift the icing over the cake (Fig. i).
3. Smooth the icing over the top and down the side(s) of the cake with cornfloured hands (Fig. ii). If the cake is an awkward shape, it may be necessary to cut the icing to fit, then brush any joins with water and smooth together with the fingers.
4. Trim off the excess icing at the base of the cake (Fig. iii).
5. Rub the surface of the cake with cornfloured hands to make the icing smooth (Fig. iv).
6. Knead any trimmings together and seal in clingfilm or polythene until required, or use for decorations.

ROYAL ICING

Royal icing is used for wedding and celebration cakes. It sets hard, keeps well and protects the cake from drying out. It is very important to produce a good royal icing—this will help to achieve a beautiful cake.

Ensure that all your equipment is clean and free from grease before you start.

Glycerine may be added to the royal icing to soften it and make the cake easier to cut. If a tiered cake is to be made, however, it is better to omit the glycerine, to achieve a harder icing. When making decorations it is also better to leave out the glycerine.

When the icing has been made it is essential to keep it covered with a damp cloth, such as muslin, while you are using it. Otherwise a hard crust will form on the icing, which may ruin its texture.

2 large egg whites
500 g (1 lb) icing sugar

2 tablespoons Supercook
glycerine (optional)
few drops Supercook food
colouring (optional)

1. Beat the egg whites lightly. Gradually sift in the icing sugar, mixing well.
2. When half the sugar is added, beat in the glycerine if using.
3. Continue adding the icing sugar until the icing reaches the correct consistency (see below).
4. Cover with clingfilm and a damp cloth until required.

Makes a 500 g (1 lb) quantity

ROYAL ICING CONSISTENCY

When making royal icing add the icing sugar gradually to achieve the correct consistency. If the icing becomes too stiff, add more egg white.

Stiff icing—termed 'stiff peak'—is always used for piping. A slightly softer royal icing—termed 'soft peak'—should be used to cover cakes for flat or peaked icing.

Stiff peak icing consistency

When a wooden spoon is drawn out of the royal icing a fine sharp upright point should form.

Soft peak icing consistency

When a wooden spoon is drawn out of the royal icing a fine point should form which curls over at the tip.

TO COVER A CAKE WITH ROYAL ICING

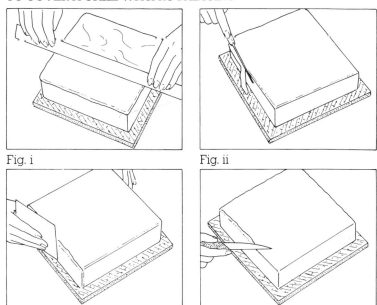

Fig. i

Fig. ii

Fig. iii

Fig. iv

Place half the icing on top of the marzipanned cake. Spread over the surface with a palette knife, pressing down to squash out air bubbles. To smooth, draw an icing ruler at an angle towards you over the cake (Fig. i). Remove surplus icing from the edge with a knife. (Fig. ii). Leave to dry before coating the side(s).

To coat the side of a round cake: Place the cake on a turntable. Spread the remaining icing around the cake with a small palette knife. Using an icing scraper at a 45° angle to the side of the cake, smooth the side in one go, turning the turntable with the other hand. Remove surplus icing from the edges with a knife. Leave to dry.

To coat the sides of a square cake: Spread the icing over 2 opposite sides with a small palette knife. Smooth with an icing scraper at a 45° angle, coming straight off at the corners (Fig. iii). Remove surplus icing with a knife. Leave to dry, then repeat on 2 remaining sides.

When the icing is completely dry, remove any rough edges with a sharp knife (Fig. iv). Apply another 1 or 2 coats, making sure each coat is dry before adding the next. Leave to dry before decorating.

USING A TEMPLATE

Many designs need to be drawn accurately to scale. The easiest way to do this and achieve a successful finish on the cake is to make a template, as follows.

Draw the letters or design on a piece of greaseproof paper cut to the exact size of the top of the cake. Place on the icing, securing with pins. Using a pin, follow the line of the design and prick through at close intervals onto the icing. Remove the paper and pipe the design onto the cake over the pin pricks.

TO MAKE A STAR TEMPLATE FOR A ROUND CAKE

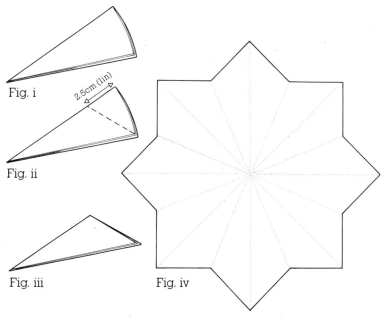

Fig. i

2.5cm (1in)

Fig. ii

Fig. iii   Fig. iv

1. Cut out a circle of paper to fit the top of the cake.
2. Fold the circle in half four times, creasing well each time, to make a thin cone shape (Fig. i).
3. Measure 2.5 (1 inch) in from the wide end, along the folded edge and mark with a pencil. Draw a diagonal line to meet the open edge (Fig. ii).
4. Cut along the marked line with a pair of scissors (Fig. iii).
5. Open out the template (Fig. iv) and transfer to the top of the cake as described above.

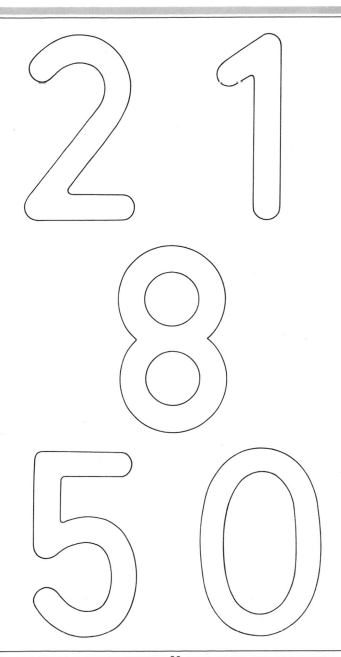

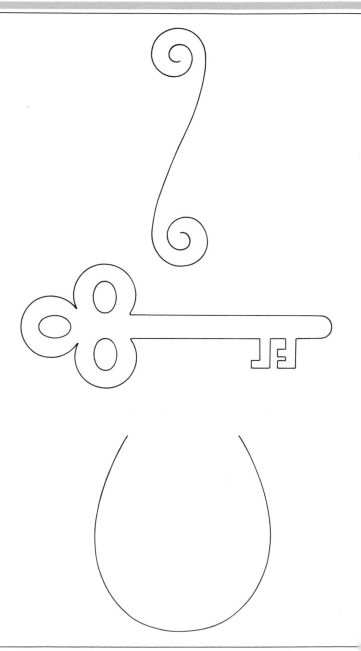

INDEX

Photography: Clive Streeter
Food preparation for photography: Alison Birch (pages 9, 13, 16–17, 25), Carole Handslip (pages 4–5, 28–9, 33, 37, 40–1, 45, 53, 57, 85), Janice Murfitt (pages 60–1, 65, 69, 73, 77)
Stylist: Gina Carminati
Line drawings: Craig Austin
Typeset by Rowland Phototypesetting Limited
Printed and bound by Blantyre Press Company Limited (Glasgow)